African Newspapers
in the

African Newspapers in the Library of Congress

Second Edition

Compiled by
John Pluge, Jr.

Serial and Government Publications Division
Research Services

Library of Congress • Washington • 1984

Library of Congress Cataloging in Publication Data

Library of Congress. Serial & Government Publications
Division.
African newspapers in the Library of Congress.

Bibliography: p.
Includes index.
Supt. of Docs. no.: LC 6.9:Af8
1. African newspapers—Bibliography—Catalogs.
2. Library of Congress—Catalogs. I. Pluge, John.
II. Title.
Z6959.Z9L53 1984 [PN5450]   015.68′035   84-600992
ISBN 0-8444-0457-8

For sale by the Superintendent of Documents, U.S. Government Printing Office,
Washington, D.C. 20402

Contents

Preface   vii

Abbreviations and Other
    Symbols   ix

Newspaper Entries   1

Algeria   1
Angola   5
Benin   7
Botswana   8
Burundi   9
Cameroon   10
Cape Verde   12
Central African Republic   13
Chad   14
Congo   15
Djibouti   17
Egypt   18
Equatorial Guinea   29
Ethiopia   30
Gabon   33
Gambia   34
Ghana   35
Guinea   39
Guinea—Bissau   40
Ivory Coast   41
Kenya   42
Lesotho   46
Liberia   47
Libya   50

Madagascar   54
Malawi   59
Mali   60
Mauritania   61
Mauritius   62
Morocco   65
Mozambique   74
Namibia   76
Niger   77
Nigeria   78
Réunion   86
Rwanda   87
São Tomé and Principe   88
Senegal   89
Seychelles   90
Sierra Leone   91
Somalia   92
South Africa   94
Sudan   107
Swaziland   111
Tanzania   112
Togo   116
Tunisia   117
Uganda   120
Upper Volta   124
Zaire   125
Zambia   129
Zimbabwe   132

Title Index   135

Preface

The continuing interest in African newspapers as a reference source, especially for political and economic developments in Africa, has prompted the Serial and Government Publications Division to revise this comprehensive list of the Library of Congress's extensive holdings of African newspapers. This updates the Library's holdings cited in the November 1977 edition. There are 931 African newspaper titles listed of which some 322 are newly reported titles. These holdings include both hard copy and positive microfilm. We have not provided the location of master negative microfilm, for that information is available in *Newspapers in Microform, Foreign Countries, 1948-1972, 1973-1977* (Washington: Library of Congress, 1973, 1978) and its annual supplements.

The fifty-two countries covered by this work are listed alphabetically with each title similarly arranged under the city of publication. The frequency of publication, when known, is given by a symbol after each title, and, where available, the date of establishment is also supplied.

The dates of holdings are the inclusive dates of the issues and are indicated in abbreviated form. For example: 1936-1956. May 3-Oct. 31 indicates that the Library has the issues for the title, in complete or almost complete form, for the period of May 3, 1936, to and including October 31, 1956. The reader should always keep in mind that in the majority of cases the Library's microfilm holdings of African newspapers are incomplete. For example, the microfilm holdings of *L'Essor* (Bamako, Mali), a title filmed at this library, are listed as 1961 + . Though most of the months for the years since 1961 are included on film, there are some years where whole weeks and even some months are missing from the filmed file. In order to know what periods are missing from any given file the reader is encouraged to contact the Serial Division directly.

Generally the language of publication is omitted, except when:

(a) the language varies from the language, or languages, most generally used for publications in the country;

(b) the language of publication varies from the language of publication of the title, or the title does not indicate clearly the language of publication;

(c) the publication is issued in two or more languages;

(d) the title is in Arabic, Amharic (or other languages of Ethiopia), or Yiddish. The reader should keep in mind that newspapers published in these languages are held in the African and Middle Eastern Division rather than in the general newspaper collection. The Chinese language title of Mauritius is available in the Asian Division.

Also when the note "In the vernacular" is used it is an indication that the language has not been identified.

John Pluge, Jr., Assistant to the Head of the Newspaper Section, Serial and Government Publications Division, compiled this bibliography with the invaluable assistance of Bernard A. Bernier, Frank J. Carroll, and Kathleen Y. Hinkle, also of the Serial Division. The Serial Division is indebted to the following Library employees without whose aid this work could not have been accomplished: George D. Selim, Near East Section, Beverly Ann Gray, African Section, and Myron M. Weinstein, Hebraic Section, African and Middle Eastern Division; and James C. Armstrong, Field Director, Library of Congress Office, Nairobi, Kenya.

The information in this guide is complete through June 1983.

DONALD F. WISDOM, CHIEF
Serial and Government
Publications Division

Abbreviations and Other Symbols

b-w.	biweekly
d.	daily
est.	established
irreg.	irregular
m.	monthly
(m).	mutilated
s-m.	semimonthly
s-w.	semiweekly
t-m.	trimonthly
t-w.	triweekly
w.	weekly
4w.	4 times weekly
5w.	5 times weekly
6w.	6 times weekly
+	The plus sign indicates that the title is currently received and is complete from the latest year given.
( )	Parentheses surrounding a date indicate that the date is supplied or inferred from other sources.
(Sample file)	The issues so indicated are a part of a worldwide collection that is in the custody of the Newspaper Section.
(Sample issue)	The issues so indicated are a part of the collection of the Near East Section, African and Middle Eastern Division.

More than one abbreviation denoting frequency of publication, following the title, indicates successive changes of periodicity.

Newspaper Entries

Algeria

Algiers

Alger ce soir. d. est. June? 1964.
    1965. July 1 (sample file).

Alger républicain. d. est. Oct. 1, 1938.
    Note: Resumed publication Oct. 2, 1943, after three-year suspension.
    United with *Le Peuple* to form *El-Moudjahid.*
    1943–1944. Oct. 2–Dec. 31.
    1945–1955. Mar.–Sept. 12 (microfilm).
    1962–1964. Oct. 25–Dec. 31 (microfilm).
    1965. Apr. 1–June 18.

Alger-soir. d. est. May 3, 1942.
    1942. May 3.

al-Baṣa'ir.
    Note: In Arabic.
    1936–1939. Mar. 27–July 28 (microfilm).
    1947–1956. July 25–Apr. 6 (microfilm).

al-Chaab. d. est. Sept. 19, 1962.
    Note: In French. Continued by *Le Peuple.*
    1962–1963. Nov. 1–Mar. 20 (microfilm).

Courrier de l'Algérie. t-w., 4w. est. Dec. 1, 1861.
    1861–1862. Dec.–Dec.

La Dépêche algérienne. d. est. 1884.
    1942. Nov. 3, 4, 6, 7.
    1943–1945. Jan. 1–Jan. 1.

La Dépêche d'Algérie. d. est. 1945?
    Note: Ceased publication Sept. 17, 1963.
    1962–1963. Mar. 1–Sept. 17 (incomplete microfilm).

1

La Dépêche quotidienne d'Algérie. d. est. Dec. 1, 1949.
            1955. Sept. 27.

Dernière heure. d. est. 1946?
            1955. Sept. 24.

Les Dernières nouvelles. d. est. 1939?
            1943–1945. Jan.–Feb.

Dimanche matin. est. 1954?
            1956–1961. Jan. 1–Apr. 16.

L'Echo d'Alger. d. est. 1912.
    Note: Ceased publication Apr. 25, 1961.
            1912. Nov. 24
            1941–1942. Dec. 15–Jan. 15.
            1942–1946. July–June (fairly complete).
            1946. Sept. 1/2.
            1948. Aug. 18.
            1950. Feb. 18–Dec. 30 (incomplete).
            1951. Jan. 2, 24–Feb. 22, Sept. 15, Oct. 12.
            1952 (incomplete).
            1953–1954.
            1955. July–Nov.
            1956–1961. Jan.–Apr. 25 (microfilm).

Le Journal d'Alger. d. est. Oct. 22, 1946.
    Note: Title (May 17)–(Sept. 29), 1950, *Le Journal.*
            1950. May 17–Nov. 21.
            1951. Jan. 24–Feb. 22, Sept. 23, 24.
            1953.
            1958.
            1961–1962. June–Mar. (incomplete microfilm).

Moniteur algérien. w. est. Jan. 27, 1832.
            1845. Jan. 10.

El-Moudjahid. d. est. June 22, 1965.
    Note: In French. Formed by the merger of *Alger républicain* and *Le Peuple.*
            1965. June 22+ (microfilm).

al-Mujahid. b-w., w.
    Note: In Arabic.
            1961. Jan.–Dec. (microfilm).

Les Nouvelles. d. est. 1900.
      1901–1903. July 1–Oct. 20.

Le Peuple. d.
  Note: Continues *al-Chaab*. United with *Alger républicain* to form *El-Moud-jahid*.
      1963–1965. Mar. 21–June 21 (microfilm).

Sahara libre. irreg. est. Nov. 13, 1975.
      1975. Nov. 13+ (microfilm).

al-Sha'b. d. est. 1962.
  Note: In Arabic.
      1971–1973 (microfilm).
      1975+ (microfilm).

Le Télégramme algérien. d. est. 1896.
      1899–1900. Dec. 16–Nov. 20.

al-Thawrah wa-al-'amal.
  Note: In Arabic.
      1970. Jan. 27 (sample issue).

Bône

La Dépêche de l'est. d. est. 1887.
      1941. Oct. 10–16 (m).
      1943.
      1944–1945 (incomplete).

Constantine

La Dépêche de Constantine et de l'est algérien. d. est. 1908.
  Note: Title May 1, 1943–June 26, 1946, *Dépêche de Constantine*.
      1943–1946. May 1–June 26.
      1954. Jan.–June.

al-Naṣr. d. est. 1963.
  Note: In Arabic.
      1971. Nov. 16 (sample issue).

Oran

L'Echo d'Oran. d. est. 1844.
　　　　1941–1942. Oct.–Aug. (incomplete).
　　　　1942–1946. Oct. 1–Jan. 31.
　　　　1946–1956. Feb.–Dec. (microfilm).

Echo-dimanche. est. Feb. 1, 1948.
　　Note: Title formerly *L'Echo du dimanche.*
　　　　1948. Feb. 1.
　　　　1956–1962. Jan. 1–June 24.

Echo-soir. d.
　　　　1955. Sept. 27.

al-Jumhūrīyah. d. est. 1963.
　　Note: In Arabic.
　　　　1978–1979. Feb. 9–May 5 (incomplete microfilm).
　　　　Current issues held for one year only.

Oran républicain. d.
　.　　1941. Aug. 18–Dec. 31 (fairly complete).
　　　　1942–1946. Jan.–Apr. (incomplete).
　　　　1950–1953. Jan.–Sept. (microfilm).
　　　　1953. Oct.–Dec.

La République. d. est. 1963.
　　　　1973. June–Dec. (microfilm).

Angola

Benguela

O Intransigente. s-w. est. 1937?
    1955. Oct. 19.

Jornal de Benguela. s-w. est. 1912?
    1955. Sept. 26.
    1963. Apr. 4–Dec. 30 (microfilm).

Bié

A Voz do Bié. w. est. 1961?
    1965. Apr. 15 (sample file).

Huambo

O Planalto. s-w.
    1974–1975. July–June (incomplete microfilm).

O Voz do planalto. w. est. 1931?
    1953. Dec. 3.

Lobito

O Lobito. s-w., d. est. 1931?
    1955. Oct. 14.
    1965. Apr. 14 (sample file).

Luanda

ABC Diário de Angola. d. est. 1959.
  Note: Ceased publication May 28, 1971.
    1965. Apr. 1, May 2, 3 (sample file).

Angola norte. w. est. 1947?
    1965. Apr. 10 (sample file).

O Apostolado. b-w. est. 1936?
    1963. Jan.–Dec. (microfilm)
    1965. Apr. 14 (sample file).

O Comercio. d. est. 1935?
        1949–1951. Oct. 4–Dec. 29 (incomplete).
        1952–1953. July–June.
        1961–1969. Sept.–Dec. (incomplete microfilm)
        1974–1975. Apr.–June (microfilm).

Diário de Luanda. d. est. 1931?
  Note: Ceased publication Nov. 20, 1976.
        1950. Aug. 15.
        1951. Sept. 16–Dec. 31.
        1952–1953. July–Aug. (fairly complete).
        1954–1955. May–June (incomplete).
        1955. Dec. 15–20, 22–31.
        1956. Jan. 2–Nov. 25 (incomplete).
        1959–1960 (fairly complete).
        1961–1974. Jan.–Sept. (microfilm).
        1976. May 1–Nov. 20 (microfilm).

Ecos de Angola. t-w. est. 1953.
        1955. Oct. 19.

Jornal de Angola. d.
  Note: Continues *A Provincia de Angola*.
        1975. July 1+

A Provincia de Angola. d. est. 1923.
  Note: Continued by *Jornal de Angola*, July 1, 1975.
        1949. Aug. 15, Dec. 31.
        1950. Aug. 15, Dec. 31.
        1951. Sept. 17–Dec. 31.
        1952–1953. July–Aug.
        1953. Dec.
        1954. July 1–Nov. 29.
        1955–1956. May 1–Nov. 26 (fairly complete).
        1959. (fairly complete).
        1961–1963. Aug. 18–Dec. 31 (microfilm).
        1971–1972. Jan.–Dec. (microfilm).
        1974–1975. June–June 29 (microfilm).

Vitoria certa. t-m? est. 1975?
  Note: Place of publication uncertain.
        1975. Nov. 29, Dec. 10, 20 (sample file).

Uíge

Jornal do Congo. w.
        1961–1962. Jan.–July (incomplete microfilm).
        1970–1973. July–Dec. (incomplete microfilm).

Benin

Cotonou

Daho express. d. est. 1969.
　Note: In French. Ceased publication Oct. 23, 1975. Succeeded by
　　Ehuzu.
　　　1969. July 28 [vol. 1, no. 0] (sample file)
　　　1970. Sept. 1–29.
　　　1972–1975. Jan.–Oct. 23 (microfilm).

Ehuzu. d. est. Oct. 24, 1975.
　Note: In French. Succeeds *Daho express.*
　　　1975. Oct. 24 + (microfilm).

Porto-Novo

L'Aube nouvelle du Dahomey. w. est. Nov. 1960.
　　　1960–1961. Dec. 8–Dec. 30 (incomplete).
　　　1968–1969. Jan. 7–Jan. 5 (incomplete microfilm).

France-Dahomey. s-w., w.
　　　1955. Nov. 11.
　　　1960. Oct. 13, 20.

Botswana

Gaborone

Daily news (Dikgang Tsa Gompieno). d. est. 1964.
    Note: In English and Tswana.
            1975+ (microfilm).

Therisanyo. bi-m., m.
    Note: In English and Tswana.
            1965-1970. Jan.-May (microfilm).

Burundi

Bujumbura

La Chronique congolaise. w., s-w. est. July 1, 1948.
        1948-1949. July-Dec.
        1950 (incomplete).
        1951-1954 (fairly complete).
        1955. Jan. 1, 8-Feb. 23.
        1957-1959. Apr. 13-Dec. 31 (fairly complete).
        1960 (incomplete).

Dépêche du Ruanda-Urundi. w.
        1955. Dec. 30.

Le Renouveau du Burundi. d. est. Apr. 13, 1978.
    Note: Succeeds Agence burundaise de presse. *Bulletin quotidien—Agence burundaise de presse.*
        1978. Apr. 13 + (microfilm).

Temps nouveau d'Afrique. w. est. 1955?
        1960-1961 (incomplete).
        1962. Jan.-May 20 (microfilm).

Cameroon

Cameroon chronicle.
       1977. May 28 (sample file).

Douala

Cameroon panorama international.
       1977. Nov. 2/9 (sample file).

La Presse du Cameroun. w., t-w., d.
   Note: Title until Mar. 7, 1955, *L'Eveil du Cameroun*. Ceased publication
      June 29, 1974. Succeeded by the *Cameroon tribune*, Yaoundé.
       1950–1951. Mar. 18–Dec. 29 (incomplete).
       1952. July 26.
       1953. July 2–Dec. 26 (incomplete).
       1954–1955. Jan. 23–Mar. 5 (fairly complete).
       1955. Apr. 18–Nov. 30 (incomplete).
       1956–1960 (fairly complete).
       1961.
       1962–1974. Jan.–June 29 (microfilm).

Victoria

Cameroon times. 4w., t-w. est. 1960.
       1965–1968. Nov. 20–May 30 (incomplete microfilm).
       1973. Aug. 4+ (microfilm).

The Guardian. w. est. Jan. 31/Feb. 7, 1982.
       1982. Jan. 31/Feb. 7 (sample file).

Week-ender.
       1976. Jan. 10/16 (sample file).

Yaoundé

Cameroon tribune. d. est. July 1, 1974.
   Note: In French. Succeeds *La Presse du Cameroun*, Douala.
       1974. July 1 + (microfilm).

Cameroon tribune. w.
      1977. Mar. 16 (sample file).

Le Cameroun libre. s-m. est. 1943.
  Note: Ceased publication Jan. 1958.
      1951–1955 (incomplete).

Cape Verde

Mindelo

Noticias de Cabo Verde. irreg.
        1941–1943. Nov. 29–Feb. 24.

Praia

Voz di povo. w. est. July 17, 1975.
        1977. Feb. 12+ (microfilm).

Central African Republic

Bangui

La Presse d'aujourd'hui: Bangui la so. d.
        1962. Jan. 2–June 30 (microfilm).
        1962–1966. Sept. 1–Dec. 31 (microfilm).

Soukoula.
        1975. Feb. 20 (sample file).

Terre africaine.
        1958. Nov. (sample file).

Terre africaine. w. est. Jan. 19, 1963.
        1963–1976. Jan. 19–Feb. 10 (incomplete microfilm).
        1981. Mar. 25.
        1982. Sept.

Chad

N'Djamena

Canard Déchaine. w. est. 1973.
　　　　1974. June 1, Dec. 28 (sample file).

Congo

Brazzaville

A.E.F. w. est. June 12, 1943.
    1943. July 24.

Dipanda. w.
  Note: In French. Ceased publication Oct. 10, 1967; however, a special
    issue was published for Nov. 1967.
    1963–1967. Nov.–Nov. (microfilm).

L'Équateur. d.
    1952. Mar. 4–July 20 (fairly complete).

Etumba. w.
  Note: In French.
    1969. Dec. 27+ (microfilm).

France-Afrique. w.
  Note: Incorporated in *France-équateur l'avenir*, Jan. 3, 1956.
    1951–1955. Nov. 18–May 7/14 (incomplete).

France-equateur l'avenir. t-w., d. est. Sept. 8, 1952.
  Note: Title Sept. 8, 1952–Dec. 31, 1955, *France-équateur*. Incorporated
    France-Afrique and *L'Avenir*, Jan. 3, 1956. Ceased publication Mar.
    3, 1960.
    1952. Sept. 8–Nov. 17.
    1953. Feb. 14–May 27, Sept. 12–Dec. 31.
    1954–1955 (incomplete).
    1956–1959 (microfilm).

L'Homme nouveau; kongo ya sika. w. est. Mar. 1, 1960.
  Note: In French. Ceased publication Dec. 1963.
    1960–1963. Mar.–Dec. (microfilm).

Mweti. s-w., t-w. est. 1977.
    1977–1979. Sept.–Feb. (microfilm).
    1980. Mar. + (microfilm).

Le Petit journal de Brazzaville, d. est. 1958.
    1965. Jan. 4 (sample file).

La Semaine africaine. w. est. 1952.
  Note: Title (Jan. 24, 1953)–(Feb. 18, 1956), *La Semaine de l'A.E.F.*; Dec.
    27, 1964–Dec. 25, 1977, *La Semaine*.
        1953. Jan. 24–Oct. 3 (incomplete).
        1954. Aug. 21–Oct. 9, Dec. 18, 25.
        1955. Jan. 1–Feb. 19, May 28.
        1956. Feb. 18.
        1960. Jan. + (microfilm).

Djibouti

Djibouti

La Nation Djibouti. w. est. June 29, 1980.
　Note: Succeeds *Le Réveil de Djibouti*.
　　　1980. June 29 + (microfilm).

Le Réveil de Djibouti. w.
　Note: Ceased publication June 26, 1980. Succeeded by *La Nation Dji-bouti*.
　　　1962–1980. July 7–June 26 (microfilm).

Egypt

Alexandria

Anatole. d.
  Note: In Greek.
      1949. May–Dec.
      1950. Apr. 7–14, Aug. 18–Sept. 1, Oct. 13–Dec. 31.

Cronaca. w.
  Note: In Italian.
      1955. Apr. 23.

La Gazette d'orient. w. during winter; b-w. during summer.
      1946–1948. May 26–Jan. 3 (incomplete).

al-Ḥiwār.
  Note: In Arabic.
      1976. Jan. 27 (sample issue).

L'Informateur. w.
      1955. May 27.

Le Journal d'Alexandrie et la bourse égyptienne. d.
      1951–1952. Apr. 6–Dec. 30 (incomplete).
      1953–1954. Jan.–June (fairly complete).

Journal du commerce et de la marine. d. est. 1909.
  Note: Suspended publication Dec. 1962.
      1944–1947. Apr. 21–Dec. 31 (incomplete).
      1948–1961.
      1962 (microfilm).

Le Moniteur égyptien. w. est. 1833.
      1834. Jan. 11–25 (microfilm).

Le Phare égyptien. d., t-w.
  Note: Ceased publication Aug. 11, 1965.
      1952. Feb.–Dec.
      1963–1965. Jan. 31–Aug. 11 (microfilm).

La Réforme. d. est. 1895.
      1952. Feb. 16–Dec. 31.
      1953.

La Réforme illustrée du dimanche.
Note: Ceased publication May 16, 1965.
      1963–1965. Feb. 17–May 16 (microfilm).

Tachydromos. d. est. 1882.
Note: In Greek.
      1944. Apr. 27, June 1–Oct. 26 (incomplete).
      1949. May–Dec.
      1950–1951. Sept. 13–Mar. 6 (incomplete).
      1952–1957 (incomplete).
      1962+ (microfilm).

Cairo

Actualité. w.
      1955. May 28.

al-Ahram. w., d. est. 1875.
Note: In Arabic.
      1876–1877. Aug. 5–July 31 (microfilm).
      1878–1894. Aug.–Aug. 22 (microfilm).
      1895–1896. Jan.–Dec. (microfilm).
      1900. Jan.–Dec. (microfilm).
      1907+ (microfilm).

al-Aḥrār. w. est. Nov. 14, 1977.
Note: In Arabic.
      1977. Nov. 14+ (incomplete microfilm).

al-Akhbār. d. est. 1952.
Note: In Arabic. See also *Akhbār al-yawm*.
      1961–1976. Jan.–June (microfilm).
      1977+ (microfilm).

Akhbār al-'ummāl. m.
Note: In Arabic.
      1977. July (sample issue).

Akhbār al-yawm. w. est. 1944.
Note: In Arabic. 1962–1966 microfilmed with *al-Akhbār*.
      1946–1952. Jan.–Dec. (microfilm).
      1961+ (microfilm).

al-'Alam.
   Note: In Arabic.
         1910. Mar. 7–July 31 (microfilm).

Anbā' al-Jīzah.
   Note: In Arabic.
         1963. Oct. 18 (sample issue).

Arev. d. est. 1915.
   Note: In Armenian.
         1945–1979 (microfilm).

al-Ba 'kūkah al-jadīdah.
   Note: In Arabic.
         1970. Jan. 1 (sample issue).

al-Bālagh. d.
   Note: In Arabic.
         1942–1943. July 27–Feb. (microfilm).
         1945–1946. Jan.–Feb. (incomplete microfilm).
         1946–1951. Apr.–Mar. (microfilm).
         1951–1953. June–June (microfilm).

La Bourse égyptienne. d. est. 1897?
   Note: Ceased publication Dec. 31, 1963.
         1929–1931. Dec. 12–Oct. 10.
         1943–1960.
         1961–1962 (microfilm).

Deutsche Orient-zeitung. w. est. 1953?
   Note: In German.
         1953. Feb. 7–21, June 7–Nov. 29.
         1954. Jan. 3–Mar. 14.

Echos. w. est. 1947.
   Note: In French.
         1950. June 4–25.
         1951. May 6–27.
         1952–1953. Feb. 3–Dec. 27 (incomplete).

Egyptian gazette. w, d. est. Jan. 26, 1880.
   Note: Published in Alexandria until Feb. 28, 1938.
         1900–1941. Jan. 2–Jan. 15 (microfilm).
         1943. Jan. 3+ (microfilm).

Egyptian mail. w. est. 1910.
     1945. (incomplete).
     1946–1955. Jan.–Mar.
     1955. Apr. + (microfilm).

Egyptian standard. d. est. Mar. 3, 1907.
  Note: See also *L'Etendard égyptien.*
     1907–1908. Mar. 3–Apr. 8.

L'Etendard égyptien. d. est. Mar. 2, 1907.
  Note: See also the *Egyptian standard.*
     1907–1908. Mar. 2–Dec. 29.

al-Fidā' al-jadīd.
  Note: In Arabic.
     1977. Feb. 7 (sample issue).

al-Ḥaqā'iq.
  Note: In Arabic.
     1964. Oct. 13 (sample issue).

Housaper. d.
  Note: In Armenian.
     1945–1978 (microfilm).
     1979 +

al-Ḥurrīyah.
  Note: In Arabic.
     1975. July 15 (sample issue).

al-I'lām.
  Note: In Arabic.
     1885–1889. Jan. 11–Jan. 3 (microfilm).

al-I'tidāl.
  Note: In Arabic.
     1910. Mar. 20 (sample issue).

al-Jarīdah al-tijārīyah al-Miṣrīyah. w. est. 1921.
  Note: In Arabic.
     1962 (incomplete).
     1963 + (microfilm).

Jarīdat Miṣr.
    Note: In Arabic.
                1977–1978. June 28–Sept. 19 (microfilm).

al-Jihād.
    Note: In Arabic.
                1933. Jan.–Dec. (microfilm).
                1935. Jan.–Apr. (microfilm).
                1937. Jan–June (microfilm).

Le Journal d'Égypte. d. est. 1936.
                1944–1946. Jan. 18–Dec. 30 (incomplete).
                1947–1959. Jan.–Apr.
                1962+ (microfilm).

Le Journal égyptien. d.
                1897. Jan.–June.

Jugoslovenski glasnik. w.
    Note: Issued alternately in Serbian and Croatian.
                1941–1942. Aug. 23–June 20.

al-Jumhūrīyah. d. est. 1953.
    Note: In Arabic.
                1953. Dec. 7+ (microfilm).

Kawkab al-Sharq.
    Note: In Arabic.
                1926. Jan.–Apr. (microfilm).
                1927–1928. Jan.–Dec. (microfilm).
                1933. Jan.–Dec. (microfilm).
                1937. Jan.–Dec. (microfilm).

al-Kūrah.
    Note: In Arabic.
                1963. Nov. 1 (sample issue).

Lisān al-'Arab.
    Note: In Arabic.
                1894–1897. Aug.–Dec. (microfilm).

al-Liwā' al-Miṣrī.
    Note: In Arabic.
                1921–1923. Aug. 23–Oct. 24 (microfilm).
                1924–1925. May 13–May 3 (microfilm).

al-Maʿāhid al-ʿulyā: jarīdat al-ṭalabah.
Note: In Arabic.
    1967. Apr. (sample issue).

al-Masāʾ. d.
Note: In Arabic.
    1962–1963. Jan.–Dec. (microfilm).
    1964–1967. July–Jan. (microfilm).

Le Messager. w.
Note: In French and Arabic.
    1964+ (microfilm).

Miṣr. d.
Note: In Arabic.
    1962–1966. Jan. 2–Feb. 3 (microfilm).

Miṣr al-Fatāh.
Note: In Arabic.
    1908–1909. Dec. 1–May 31 (microfilm).

Miṣr al-Kinānah.
Note: ·In Arabic.
    1977. May 1 (sample issue).

al-Miṣri. d.
Note: In Arabic.
    1944–1953. Jan.–Sept. (microfilm).

al-Mujtamaʿ.
Note: In Arabic.
    1970. Mar. 4 (sample issue).

al-Muqaṭṭam. d.
Note: In Arabic.
    1889. Feb. 14–Oct. 17 (microfilm).
    1910. June 18–Sept. 18 (microfilm).
    1925. Apr. 8–July 10 (microfilm).
    1939. May 9–Aug. 26 (microfilm).
    1940–1952. Jan.–Sept. (microfilm).

al-Mushīr.
Note: In Arabic.
    1894–1897. Nov. 1–Aug. 6 (microfilm).

L'Observateur. d.
        1951–1957. July 3–Aug. 3 (incomplete).

Ho Paroikas. d.
   Note: In Greek.
        1954. Dec. 12.

La Patrie. d.
        1928–1929. June 17–June (microfilm).
        1929–1930. Oct.–Oct. (microfilm).
        1934–1953. Nov.–June (microfilm).

Phos. d. est. 1896.
   Note: In Greek.
        1955. Feb. 24.
        1962+ (microfilm).

Progrès-dimanche. w.
        1962+ (microfilm).

Le Progrès égyptien. d. est. 1890.
        1948. July–Dec.
        1949. June 28–July 13.
        1951. July–Dec. (fairly complete).
        1952–1953.
        1954 (fairly complete).
        1955–1959 Feb. 25–Apr. 30 (incomplete).
        1962+ (microfilm).

al-Qāfilah/Caravan.
   Note: In Arabic and English.
        1972. Mar. 6 (sample issue).

al-Qāhirah. d. est. 1953.
   Note: In Arabic.
        1953–1957. Dec.–Dec. (microfilm).

al-Qūwāt al-musallaḥah.
   Note: In Arabic.
        1970–1973. Feb. 25–Dec. 24 (microfilm).

al-Ra'y al-'Āmm.
   Note: In Arabic.
        1894. Nov. 7 (microfilm).
        1896. Sept. 11–Nov. 13 (microfilm).
        1897. Jan. 8–Dec. 12 (microfilm).

Le Réveil.
>1925-1931. Dec. 27-July 23 (microfilm).

al-Ṣadāqah.
>Note: In Arabic.
>1962-1967. Sept. 6-Mar. 30 (microfilm).

Ṣawt al-Hind.
>Note: In Arabic.
>1963. Nov. 15 (sample issue).

Ṣawt al-jāmi'ah.
>Note: In Arabic.
>1972-1976. Dec. 25-Apr. 12 (incomplete).
>Current issues held for one year only.

Ṣawt al-sha'b al-Lībī.
>Note: In Arabic.
>1977. Jan. 16-Sept. 11 (sample issues).

Ṣawt al-ṭullāb.
>Note: In Arabic.
>1975. Apr. (sample issue).

Ṣawt al-'ummāl.
>Note: In Arabic.
>1964. Aug. 15 (sample issue).

Ṣawt Ḥulwān.
>Note: In Arabic.
>1976. Apr. 24 (sample issue).

al-Sha'b. d.
>Note: In Arabic.
>1910. Mar. 21-May 19 (microfilm).

al-Sha'b.
>Note: In Arabic.
>1957. Jan. 1 (sample issue).

al-Shabāb al-'Arabī.
>Note: In Arabic.
>1966. Dec. 12 (sample issue).

Shabāb al-Azhar.
   Note: In Arabic.
         1976. Apr. 16 (sample issue).

al-Ṣiḥāfah.
   Note: In Arabic.
         1966. May 24 (sample issue).

al-Sinimā wa-al-funūn.
   Note: In Arabic.
         1977. Jan. 3–Aug. 29 (microfilm).

al-Siyāsah. d. est. 1922.
   Note: In Arabic.
         1922–1924. Oct. 30–Aug. 31 (microfilm).
         1925. May 1–Sept. 4 (microfilm).
         1926–1927. Oct. 31–Aug. 30 (microfilm).
         1928. May–Aug. (microfilm).
         1932–1934. Feb. 26–Aug. 13 (Supps. only-microfilm).

al-Siyāsah al-Usbūʻīyah. w. est. 1926.
   Note: In Arabic.
         1926–1931. Mar. 13–Jan. 31 (microfilm).
         1937–1938. Jan. 16–Dec. 31 (microfilm).

al-Siyāsī.
   Note: In Arabic.
         1977. May 15+ (microfilm).

al-Taʻāwun. w.
   Note: In Arabic.
         1963–1966. Feb. 3–Dec. 31 (microfilm).
         1974–1976. July 1–Dec. 31 (microfilm).
         1977–1979. Jan. 4–Mar. 27 (incomplete microfilm).

al-Taʻāwun: Jarīdat al-Fallāḥīn. w.
   Note: In Arabic.
         1962–1974. Jan. 2–June 30 (microfilm).

Taʻāwun al-ṭalabah.
   Note: In Arabic.
         1973. Mar. 25 (sample issue).

Tchahakir. w. est. 1949.
   Note: In Armenian.
         1964+ (microfilm).

The Times of Egypt. d.
> Note: Issue of Sept. 6, 1884, is in English, French and Arabic; issue of
> May 8, 1885, is in English and French.
>> 1884. Sept. 6.
>> 1885. May 8.

al-Ṭullāb.
> Note: In Arabic.
>> 1968. Oct. 15 (sample issue).

al-ʿUmmāl. m., w. est. Oct. 1966.
> Note: In Arabic.
>> 1966. Oct. 5+ (microfilm).

La Voix de l'orient. w.
>> 1953. Dec. 24.

al-Wafd al-Miṣrī. d. est. 1938.
> Note: In Arabic.
>> 1938. Apr. 1–May 31 (microfilm).

Waṭanī. w.
> Note: In Arabic.
>> 1962–1968. Jan. 7–Sept. 15 (microfilm).
>> 1970. Jan. 4–Aug. 30 (microfilm).

al-Ẓāhir.
> Note: In Arabic.
>> 1903–1904. Nov. 12–Nov. 30 (microfilm).
>> 1905–1908. Oct. 19–Apr. 23 (microfilm).

Ismailia

al-Qanāh.
> Note: In Arabic.
>> 1977. Feb. 20 + (incomplete microfilm).

Port Said

Būr Saʿīd.
> Note: In Arabic.
>> 1961. May 16 (sample issue).

Neos syndesmos. w.
> Note: In Greek.
>> 1943. Apr. 17, 24.

Suez

al-Waʻy.
  Note: In Arabic.
           1975. June (sample issue).

Tanta

al-Aḥrār.
  Note: In Arabic.
           1976. Aug. (sample issue).

al-Shabāb al-ishtirākī.
  Note: In Arabic.
           1968. Mar. 15 (sample issue).

Equatorial Guinea

Malabo

Ebano. t-w., d.
  Note: Suspended publication for a 23-month period to Jan. 1, 1943
        1943-1944. Jan. 1-Feb. 15 (incomplete microfilm).
        1960 (fairly complete).

Ebano. irreg. est. Aug. 3, 1980.
        1980. Aug. 3 +

Hoja del Lunes de Fernando Poo.
        1967. Nov. 27 (sample file).
        1971. Apr. 12 (sample file).

Unidad de la Guinea Ecuatorial. s-w.
        1974. Jan. 16-23 (sample file).

Ethiopia

Addis Ababa

Addis-Soir. d.
  Note: Ceased publication Sept. 11, 1975. Succeeded by *Le Progrès
    socialiste.*
        1968–1975. Jan.–Sept. 11 (microfilm).

'Adis Zaman. d.
  Note: In Amharic.
        1940–1966. (incomplete).
        1967–1973. Jan.–Sept. 9 (fairly complete).
        1973–1981. Sept. 11–Sept. 10 (microfilm).
        1981. Sept.12 +

Aimiro. w.
  Note: In Amharic.
        1926–1927. Sept. 11–Sept. 10.

al-'Alam. w.
  Note: In Arabic.
        1975 + (incomplete microfilm).

Barisā. w. est. 1976.
  Note: In Oromo. Frequency varies: monthly.
        1976 +

Correspondance d'Ethiopie. irreg. est. 1927.
        1927. Aug. 10–31.

Corriere dell'Impero.
        1937–1938. Jan. 3–July 13 (incomplete).

Le Courrier d'Ethiopie. w.
        1926–1927. Aug. 10–Sept. 30.

Ethiopian herald. w., d. est. July 3, 1943.
        1943–1951. July 3–Dec. 29.
        1952–1955 (incomplete).
        1956. June 23 + (microfilm).

Lumière et paix. w.
  Note: In Amharic.
        1927. Jan. 6–Sept. 29.

Le Progrès socialiste. w. est. Sept. 13, 1975.
  Note: Succeeds *Addis-Soir.* Ceased publication Oct. 8, 1977.
        1975–1977. Sept. 13–Oct. 8 (microfilm).

Sareto 'adar. s-m. est. June 19, 1980.
  Note: In Amharic. Frequency varies.
        1980. June 19 +

Voice of Ethiopia. d.
  Note: In English and Amharic. Separate English and Amharic editions
        published beginning Sept. 14, 1961. Ceased publication Mar. 24,
        1969.
        1957–1959. Jan.–June.
        1959–1969. July–Mar. 24 (microfilm).

Yazāréyutu 'Ityopyā. w.
  Note: In Amharic.
        1955 + (incomplete).

Asmara

Eritrean daily news. est. June 17, 1941.
  Note: In English and Italian. Separate English and Italian editions pub-
        lished beginning sometime between June 22 and Oct. 18, 1944.
        See *Il Quotidiano Eritreo.* Ceased publication Nov. 4, 1947. Suc-
        ceeded by *Eritrean daily bulletin.*
        1942. Feb. 3
        1944. Jan.–Apr., June 21, 22, Oct. 18, Dec. 23–31.
        1945–1947. Jan.–Oct.

Giornale dell'Eritrea. d.
  Note: Ceased publication Jan. 31, 1975.
        1952–1953. May 22–Dec. (fairly complete).
        1954–1955.
        1967–1975. Apr.–Jan. (microfilm).

Hebrat. t-w.
  Note: In Tigrinya and Arabic. Added title in Arabic: *al-Waḥdah.* Fre-
        quency varies: daily. Weekly edition entitled: *'Ityopyā.*
        1968–1972. Sept.–Dec. (incomplete).
        1973–1977 (incomplete microfilm).
        1978 +

'Itoṗyā. w.
  Note: In Tigrinya. Weekly edition of *Hebrat*.
            1947-1971. (incomplete).
            1972-1976. Sept.-Apr. (fairly complete).
            1978 +

al-Jarīdah al-'Arabīyah al-usbū'īyah.
  Note: In Arabic.
            1948-1951. Jan. 1-Dec. 31 (microfilm).

Il Quotidiano Eritreo. est. 1944.
  Note: Italian edition of *Eritrean daily news*. Suspended publication Feb. 1-
            Mar. 5, 1975. Ceased publication Sept. 11, 1976. Succeeded by *Il
            Settimanale Eritreo*.
            1944-1946. Dec. 28-Dec. 31.
            1947 (fairly complete).
            1948-1952.
            1953 (incomplete).
            1954. Sept.-Dec.
            1955-1956 (incomplete).
            1960. Mar.-Dec. (incomplete).
            1961. Jan. 2-Dec. 15 (microfilm).
            1968-1976. Jan.-Sept. 11 (microfilm).

Il Settimanale Eritreo. w. est. Sept. 18, 1976.
  Note: Succeeds *Il Quotidiano Eritreo*. Ceased publication Apr. 16? 1977.
            1976-1977. Sept. 25-Apr. 2 (microfilm).

Gabon

Libreville

Gabon d'aujourd'hui.
   1964. Nov. 14 (sample file).

L'Union. d. est. 1975.
   1976. Jan. + (microfilm).

Gambia

Banjul

Gambia echo. w. est. 1934.
    1947–1972 (incomplete microfilm).

Gambia news bulletin. t-w. est. 1943.
    1968 + (incomplete microfilm).

Gambia outlook (In miniature). t-w.?
    1975. Oct. 27, 29, 31 (sample file).

Gambia outlook and Senegambian reporter. w., t-w. est. 1922.
    1942.
    1943 (incomplete).
    1944–1947.
    1948–1955 (fairly complete).
    1979. June 20, 29 (sample file).

Gambia times. t-w., w. est. 1981.
    1982. Jan. 9 (sample file).

Nation. fortnightly, w.
    1974–1978. Jan. 12–May 27 (incomplete microfilm).

Vanguard. w. est. Mar. 15, 1958.
    1958. Apr. 12–Nov. 22.
    1959. Jan. 3–17, Feb. 21, Mar. 14, Apr. 11–May 9, June 6, 13,
    Dec. 5.

Ghana

Accra

African morning post.
> Note: Merged with *The Ghana nationalist, Ghana daily express, Daily echo,* and *Spectator daily,* forming the *Gold Coast daily mail,* later *Ghana daily mail,* in 1956.
>> 1935. Sept. 3.
>> 1936. June 8, July 1.
>> 1953-1955. Mar. 23–Mar. 31 (incomplete).

African national times. d.
>> 1950-1951. Jan. 4–Sept. 18 (incomplete).

African spectator. w. est. Sept. 1962.
>> 1962. Dec. 8 (sample file).

Daily echo.
> Note: Succeeds the *Echo* sometime after Sept. 30, 1938, but before Jan. ·3, 1939. Merged with *The Ghana nationalist, Ghana daily express, African morning post,* and *Spectator daily,* forming the *Gold Coast daily mail,* later *Ghana daily mail,* in 1956.
>> 1953-1955. Jan. 3–Apr. 30 (incomplete).

Daily graphic. est. 1953.
> Note: Continues the *Gold Coast daily graphic.*
>> 1953-1955. May 7–Nov. 30 (incomplete).
>> 1956 + (microfilm).

Evening news. est. Mar. 3, 1958.
> Note: Ceased publication Dec. 1968.
>> 1958-1959. Mar.–Dec. (incomplete).
>> 1960-1968. Jan.–Dec. 23 (microfilm).

Ghana daily express. est. 1952.
> Note: Merged with *The Ghana nationalist, Daily echo, African morning post,* and *Spectator daily,* forming the *Gold Coast daily mail,* later *Ghana daily mail,* in 1956.
>> 1952 (incomplete).

Ghana daily mail. est. 1956.
   Note: Title 1956-Mar.? 1957, *Gold Coast daily mail.* Formed by the mer-
        ger of *The Ghana nationalist, Ghana daily express, Daily echo, African
        morning post,* and *Spectator daily.* Ceased publication.
            1957. Apr. 8-Sept. 9 (incomplete).
            1958. Jan. 29.

Ghana evening news. est. Sept. 3, 1948.
   Note: Title Sept. 3, 1948-Apr. 1952?, *Accra evening news.*
            1952-1953. May 1-Aug. 8 (incomplete).
            1953. Oct. 8-10.
            1954-1955. Jan. 27-Apr. 12 (incomplete).
            1956-1958. Oct. 15-Oct. 4 (incomplete).

Ghana star. est. 1953.
   Note: Ceased publication 1958?
            1958. Jan. 25.

Ghanaian times. d. est. Mar. 3, 1958.
   Note: Title Mar. 3-June 14, 1958, *Guinea times*; June 14, 1958-July 1,
        1960, *Ghana times.*
            1958-1961. Mar. 3-Dec.
            1962 + (microfilm).

Gold Coast commercial guardian. w.
            1953. Oct. 24.

Gold Coast daily graphic. est. 1950.
   Note: Continued by the *Daily graphic.*
            1952. July-Dec. (microfilm).

Gold Coast independent. w. est. June 8, 1918.
            1942-1943. Jan. 31-Aug. 7 (incomplete).
            1947. Dec. 6(m), 13(m), 20(m), 27(m).
            1948. Jan. 31-Oct. 9 (incomplete).

Guidance. m.
            1980. Jan. (sample file).

India news.
            1959. Jan. 15.

Mirror. w. est. 1953.
  Note: Title 1953-[June 1970], *Sunday mirror*.
        1955-1956. Feb. 6-Sept. 9 (incomplete).
        1964-1970. Nov.-June (incomplete microfilm).
        1973-1974. Sept. 21-Sept. 20 (incomplete microfilm).
        1976. Aug. + (microfilm).

Palaver. w. est. Oct. 1970.
        1975. Nov. 12/18 (sample file).

Post.
        1980. Apr./July (sample file).

Spectator daily.
  Note: Merged with *The Ghana nationalist, Ghana daily express, Daily echo*,
        and *African morning post*, forming the *Gold Coast daily mail*, later
        Ghana daily mail, in 1956.
        1942-1950. June 18-Nov. 30 (incomplete).
        1951. Jan. 2-July 23.
        1952. Jan. 16-Feb. 29.
        1953-1955. Jan.-May (incomplete).

Weekly spectator. est. 1963.
        1974. Aug. +

Cape Coast

Gold Coast news. w. est. Mar. 21, 1885.
        1885. June 6.

Gold Coast observer and weekly advertiser. est. 1932.
        1948-1951. Jan. 30-Nov. 2 (incomplete).

West African monitor. d.
        1953. May 5.

Kumasi

Ashanti pioneer. d. est. Nov. 9, 1939.
  Note: Suspended publication Oct. 8, 1962-Nov. 1966. Continued as the
        Pioneer with the resumption of publication.
        1939-1942 (incomplete microfilm).
        1946-1947. Jan. 19-Sept. 18 (incomplete microfilm).
        1948-1958 (fairly complete microfilm).
        1959-1962. Jan.-Oct. 8 (microfilm).

Ashanti sentinel. d. est. 1952.
  Note: Ceased publication during 1955.
            1953-1955. Feb. 5-Nov. 29 (incomplete).

Pioneer. d.
  Note: Continued the *Ashanti pioneer* upon the resumption of publication
            on Dec. 1, 1966. Suspended publication July 18-Nov. 1, 1972.
            1968. May 6 + (microfilm).

Obuasi

Ashanti times. s-w., w. est. 1950.
  Note: Continued as the *New Ashanti times*, in 1963.
            1953. Apr. 28.
            1957. July 23.
            1958. Jan. 11-Nov. 18 (incomplete).

Guinea

Conakry

La Guinée française. d., t.w.
  Note: Ceased publication June 5, 1954.
          1950. Mar.–Dec. (fairly complete).
          1951–1954. Jan.–June 5.

Horoya. t-w. est. Apr. 18, 1961.
  Note: In French. Succeeds *La Liberté*.
          1961. Apr. 18 + (microfilm).

Guinea—Bissau

Bissau

O Arauto. d.
  Note: Suspended publication Apr. 17–June 14, 1964. Ceased publication Jan. 1972.
          1956. Apr. 4–July 3, Nov. 28–Dec. 14.
          1960–1965. June 8–Dec. (microfilm).

Nô Pintcha. s-w. est. 1975.
          1975. Aug. 2 + (microfilm).

Voz da Guine. t-w. est. Jan. 15, 1972.
          1972–1974. Mar. 21–Sept. 7 (incomplete microfilm).

Ivory Coast

Abidjan

Abidjan-matin.
> Note: Title until Oct. 1954, *France-Afrique*. Ceased publication Dec. 8,
> 1964. Succeeded by *Fraternité-matin*.
>> 1955–1956.
>> 1957–1958 (incomplete).
>> 1959–1964. Jan.–Dec. 8 (microfilm).

La Côte d'Ivoire. d., s-w., w.
> Note: Title until sometime after Apr. 13, 1946. *La Côte d'Ivoire française
> libre*.
>> 1945. Nov. 23–Dec. 18.
>> 1946. Jan. 4–Feb. 26, Mar. 23–Apr. 13.
>> 1949–1954. Sept. 14–Nov. 3/12.
>> 1955. Aug. (no. 242).

Fraternité hebdo. est. Apr. 24, 1959.
> Note: Title Apr. 24, 1959–[Sept. 1968], *Fraternité*.
>> 1959–1968. Apr. 24–Sept. (incomplete microfilm).
>> 1970. Jan. + (microfilm).

Fraternité-matin. est. Dec. 9, 1964.
> Note: Succeeds *Abidjan-matin*.
>> 1964. Dec. 9 + (microfilm).

Kenya

Eldoret

Uasin Gishu weekly advertiser.
        1945. Sept. 13, 20.
        1946–1947. Jan. 10–Dec. 25 (incomplete).
        1948. Jan. 1–Feb. 26.

Mombasa

Coastweek. w. est. Nov. 10/16, 1978.
    Note: In English, German or Swahili.
        1978. Nov. 10/16, 17/23 (sample file).
        1980. Jan.+ (microfilm).

Kenya daily mail. est. 1927.
    Note: In English and Gujarati. Ceased publication Feb. 28, 1965.
        1942. Aug. 19(m).
        1943. Jan. 13, Apr. 28.
        1944–1945. Feb. 16–Apr. 4 (fairly complete).
        1946. Apr.–Dec.
        1947–1948 (incomplete).
        1949.
        1950–1953. Jan.–Nov. (fairly complete).
        1958–1960. July–Dec.
        1961–1963 (microfilm—In Gujarati only).
        1964 (microfilm—In English only).

Kenya daily mail; weekly edition. est. 1927.
    Note: In English and Gujarati.
        1956–1958. June 15–June 27.

Mombasa advertiser. w.
    Note: Ceased publication Sept. 28, 1974.
        1969–1974. May 17–Sept. 28 (incomplete microfilm).

Mombasa times. d. est. 1902.
    Note: Ceased publication 196?.
        1955. Aug. 27.

Nairobi

Africa samachar. w. est. 1954.
  Note: In Gujarati. Ceased publication Apr. 26, 1974.
      1968-1974. Feb. 2-Apr. 26 (incomplete microfilm).

Africa times. w. est. July 1, 1933.
  Note: In English and Gujarati. Title until sometime after June 28, 1962,
      Colonial times.
          1949-1950. Apr. 30-Dec. 30 (incomplete).
          1951-1952.
          1953-1954. Jan. 1-July 10 (incomplete).
          1956-1957. July 7-June 14.
          1957-1958. Sept. 26-Dec. 18 (incomplete).
          1959-1960 (fairly complete).
          1961-1962. Jan.-June.

Baraza. w. est. 1939.
  Note: In English and Swahili. Ceased publication Dec. 27, 1979.
          1966-1979. Jan.-Dec. (microfilm).

Chemsha bongo. t-w., w. est. July 1, 1980.
  Note: In Swahili and English. Ceased publication Jan. 25, 1981.
          1980-1981. July 3-Jan. 25 (microfilm).

Daily chronicle.
  Note: In English and Gujarati. Ceased publication June 1, 1962.
          1950-1952. Feb. 7-Dec. 31.

Daily nation. est. 1960.
  Note: See also *Sunday nation.*
          1962. June+ (microfilm).

East African standard. d. except Sun. est. 1902.
  Note: Published in Mombasa as the *African standard* until Aug. 19, 1905.
      Continued as the *Standard*, July 1, 1974.
          1942. Nov. 20(m).
          1943-1945. Mar.-June (m) (incomplete).
          1945-1949. July-Dec.
          1950-1952 (fairly complete).
          1953.
          1954-1957 (microfilm).
          1958-1959. Jan.-Oct.
          1959. Dec. 31.
          1960-1974. Jan.-June 29 (microfilm).

East African standard. w.
        1925–1926. Aug. 15–Aug. 28 (microfilm).
        1927. Jan. 1–Sept. 3 (microfilm).

Evening news. d. est. Oct. 8, 1973.
  Note: Ceased publication Aug. 28, 1974.
        1973. Dec. 21 (sample file).

Goan voice. w.
        1949–1950. July–Dec. (fairly complete).
        1951–1952.
        1953–1956. Jan.–Aug. (fairly complete).

Kenya mirror. b-m., m. est. June 1968.
  Note: Ceased publication May 1974.
        1968–1974. June–May (incomplete microfilm).

Kenya times. d. est. Apr. 5, 1983.
  Note: Succeeds the *Nairobi times*.
        1983. Apr. 5+

Mseto. w. est. Feb. 15, 1981.
  Note: In Swahili. Suspended publication Apr.-[June?] 1981.
        1981. Feb. 15–Mar. 22, July 5, Oct. 18 (microfilm).
        1982+

Nairobi times. w. est. Oct. 30, 1977.
  Note: Suspended publication Nov. 30, 1981–June 27, 1982. **Incorpo**rated *Financial times*, June 28, 1982. Ceased publication **Mar. 31,** 1983. Succeeded by the *Kenya times*.
        1977–1983. Oct. 30–Mar. 31 (microfilm).

Nyanza times.
        1965. June 18 (sample file).

Sauti ya Kanu. w.
        1961. Aug. 23–Dec. 27 (incomplete).

Sauti ya Mwafrika.
        1965. Feb. 19 (sample file).

Standard. d.
  Note: Continues the *East African Standard*.
        1974. July 1+ (microfilm).

Sunday nation. est. 1960.
  Note: Sunday edition of the *Daily nation*.
        1963. Aug. 4, Oct. 6, Dec. 29.
        1967+ (microfilm).

Sunday post. w. est. Oct. 13, 1935.
   Note: Ceased publication Sept. 8, 1974.
            1942–1952. Oct. 4–Dec. 28.
            1953–1954 (fairly complete).
            1955–1961.
            1962–1963. Jan. 14–Jan. 6 (microfilm).
            1970–1973 (microfilm).

Sunday standard. w. est. Nov. 11, 1979.
            1979. Nov. 11+ (microfilm).

Taifa weekly. est. 1960.
   Note: In Swahili. Title until Jan. 11, 1969, *Taifa Kenya*.
            1961. Aug. 26+ (microfilm).

Taifaleo. 5w. est. 1960.
   Note: In Swahili.
            1961. Aug. 21+ (microfilm).

Voice of Africa. Ṣawt al-Afrīqī. w. est. May 29, 1980.
   Note:In English. Ceased publication Feb. 19, 1981.
            1980. May 29–Dec. 11 (microfilm).

Weekend star. est. Feb. 29, 1976.
   Note: Ceased publication Apr. 18, 1976.
            1976. Feb. 29–Apr. 18 (microfilm).

Nakuru

Central Africa review. w.
   Note: Central African edition of *Kenya weekly news*.
            1954–1956. Sept. 11–Apr. 27.

Kenya weekly news. est. 1928.
   Note: Began publication as the *Nakuru advertiser*, then became the *Nakuru
            weekly news*. Published in Nairobi, Apr. 5, 1968–Sept. 26, 1969.
            Ceased publication Sept. 26, 1969.
            1943 (incomplete).
            1944–1952. Jan.–Mar. (fairly complete).
            1953. Jan.–July (incomplete).
            1954. Oct. 15.
            1955. Industrial supplement only.
            1956–1961. May–Dec.
            1962–1969. Jan.–Sept. 26 (microfilm).

Lesotho

Maseru

Lesotho news. w. est. Jan. 8, 1927.
  Note: Title until Sept. 20 or 27, 1966, *Basutoland news*. Published as a
    section of the *Ladybrand courant and border herald* (South Africa), after
    Aug. 1970.
      1956–1957. Feb. 21–July 9 (microfilm).
      1958–1970. June 24–June 2 (microfilm).

Lesotho times. w. est. May 1962.
  Note: In English and South Sotho. Title May–Dec. 1962, *Basutoland
    Newsletter*, Jan. 1963 until sometime in Aug. 1964, *The Basutoland
    times*. Ceased publication Feb. 28, 1969.
      1964–1969. Sept. 25–Feb. 28 (incomplete microfilm).

Lesotho weekly. est. Apr. 1977.
  Note: Succeeds *Koena News*.
      1980. Jan. + (microfilm).

Mochochonono. w. est. Aug. 1974.
  Note: In English and South Sotho.
      1979. Apr. 24 + (microfilm).

Mazenod

Moeletsi oa Basotho. w. est. Jan. 1933.
  Note: In South Sotho and English.
      1934. Jan. 10 + (microfilm).

Morija

Leselinyana la Lesotho. b-w. est. Nov. 1863.
  Note: In English and South Sotho.
      1975 + (microfilm).

Liberia

Gbarnga

Bong crier. w. est. 1982.
    1982. May 11 (sample file).

Monrovia

African nationalist. w.
    1940–1941. Dec. 7–Nov. 22 (incomplete microfilm).
    1942–1943.
    1944–1950. Mar. 4–Apr. 22 (incomplete).

Africa's luminary. s-m. est. Mar. 15, 1839.
    1839–1840. Mar. 15–Mar. 6
    1841. Nov. 19.

Daily observer. est. 1981.
    1981. Sept. 25+

Daily times.
    1950. Oct. 4–Dec. 14 (fairly complete).

Express. w.
    1981. Feb. 4 (sample file).

Friend. w.
    1953. Jan. 10–July (fairly complete).

Herald. w. est. 1964?
    1964. May 18 (sample file).

Independent. est. Sept. 25, 1954.
    1954. Sept. 25.

Liberia herald. m. est. May. 6, 1830.
  Note: Ceased publication in 1862.
            1830. Apr. 6, June 6.
            1831. Apr. 22, June 22, July 22.
            1832. Feb. 22–June 7.
            1833. Aug. 1, Sept. 4, Nov. 20, Dec. 24.
            1834. Jan. 24, Feb. 24, June 7–Dec. 27.
            1835. Jan. 31–Apr. 30, June 30–Oct. 31, extra Sept. 5.
            1837. May–Dec.
            1838. May–June.
            1839. Oct.
            1843. Feb. 21.

Liberia herald. b-w. est. 1930.
            1930. May 10.

Liberia herald. w. est. 1941?
            1942. Sept. 4, Oct. 23, 30, Nov. 20.
            1943. Jan. 22.

Liberian age. fortnightly, t-w., s-w. est. May 14, 1946.
            1946. May 14.
            1946–1949. Aug. 31–Nov. 15.
            1950–1954. Jan. 30–Dec. 31.
            1955. Feb. 25–Dec. 26.
            1956+ (microfilm).

Liberian inaugural. w.
            1981. Feb. 4 (sample file).

Liberian news. m.
            1920. Aug.

Liberian press. m.
            1926. Jan.

Liberian star. d. est. June 1, 1964.
  Note: Ceased publication Oct. 7, 1977.
            1964–1977. June 1–Oct. 7 (microfilm).

Listener. d. est. May 22, 1950.
  Note: Ceased publication during 1972.
            1950–1971. May 22–May 5 (microfilm).

New Liberian. w, d. est. Mar. 9, 1978.
    1978. Mar. 23+ (microfilm).

Saturday chronicle. est. Jan. 25, 1969.
    1969–1970. Feb. 1–Oct. 24 (incomplete microfilm).

The Times. w. est. July 10, 1982.
    1982. July 10 (sample file).

Weekend news.
    1980. Oct. 4 (sample file).

Weekly mirror.
    1939–1941. Jan. 27–Dec. 26 (incomplete microfilm).
    1943. Dec. 17, 24.
    1944. Sept. 8.
    1946–1947. Mar. 15–Oct. 17 (incomplete).

Whirlwind. w.
    1943. May 22, 29, June 19, 26, Aug. 14, Dec. 11, 24.
    1944. Jan. 15–June 17.
    1945. Apr. 7–May 5.

Libya

Benghazi

al-'Amal.
Note: In Arabic.
    1967. Feb. 6 (sample issue).

Barqah al-Jadīdah.
Note: In Arabic. See also *al-Ummah*.
    1946–1961. Nov. 11–Dec. (microfilm).

Cyrenaica observer. w.
    1949–1951. June 12–Dec. 23 (incomplete).

Cyrenaica weekly news. est. 1957?
Note: Suspended publication Nov. 22, 1959–Sept. 3, 1961.
    1958. May 25, July 6.
    1959. Jan. 4–Nov. 22.
    1966. July 17 (sample file).

al-Haqīqah.
Note: In Arabic.
    1966. Sept. 7 (sample issue).

Libyan times. d.
Note: Ceased publication Jan. 1972.
    1968–1972. July–Jan. 19 (microfilm).

al-Raqīb.
Note: In Arabic.
    1964. Dec. 3 (sample issue).

al-Shu'lah.
Note: In Arabic.
    1967. Oct. 21 (sample issue).

al-Ummah.
Note: In Arabic.
    1967–1969. Jan.–Aug. (microfilm).

al-Zamān.
Note: In Arabic.
    1964. June 23 (sample issue).

Sehba

al-Bilād.
  Note: In Arabic.
        1967. Dec. 25 (sample issue).

Fazzān.
  Note: In Arabic.
        1967. Apr. 10 (sample issue).

Tripoli

al-Arḍ.
  Note: In Arabic.
        1978. Dec. 26 (sample issue).

al-Ayyām.
  Note: In Arabic.
        1964. May 1 (sample issue).

Corriere di Tripoli. d.
  Note: In Italian. English section entitled *Tripoli times* published (Jan.
        28)–Apr. 20, 1943.
            1943–1944. Jan. 28–Dec. 31 (incomplete).
            1945.
            1946–1952 (incomplete).
            1953–1954.
            1955–1956 (fairly complete).
            1957 (incomplete).
            1959 (fairly complete).

al-Fajr al-Jadīd. w. est. Sept. 7, 1972.
  Note: In Arabic.
        1972. Sept. 9+ (microfilm).

al-Fātih.
  Note: In Arabic.
        1974. Dec. 7 (sample issue).

Il Giornale di Tripoli. d. est. May 10, 1960.
  Note: Ceased publication 197?.
        1960–1970. May 10–May 16 (microfilm).

al-Ḥurrīyah.
  Note: In Arabic.
          1964. May 28 (sample issue).

al-Jihād.
  Note: In Arabic.
          1976–1977. Jan. 1–June 30 (microfilm).

al-Kifāḥ.
  Note: In Arabic.
          1973. May 17 (sample issue).

al-Maydān.
  Note: In Arabic.
          1965. June 27 (sample issue).

L'Ora di Tripoli. w.
          1950–1951. Aug. 28–Dec. 31 (fairly complete).
          1952. Jan. 7, 21, Aug. 4–25, Dec. 1–29.
          1953. Jan. 5–Aug. 17 (incomplete).

al-Rā'id.
  Note: In Arabic.
          1963. Dec. 2 (sample issue).

al-Ra'y.
  Note: In Arabic.
          1973. Oct. 1 (sample issue).

Sawt al-'ummāl.
  Note: In Arabic.
          1977. Nov. 5 (sample issue).

al-Sha'b.
  Note: In Arabic.
          1970. Mar. 31 (sample issue).

al-Shurṭī.
  Note: In Arabic.
          1978. Sept. 30 (sample issue).

Sunday Ghibli.
   Note: Ceased publication.
               1954. Nov. 21.
               1960–1961. Jan. 31–Sept. 24 (incomplete).
               1962. Jan.-Mar., Dec. (incomplete).
               1966–1967. Jan.–June 4 (microfilm).

al-Taḥrīr.
   Note: In Arabic.
               1968. Aug. 1 (sample issue).

al-Ṭalīʿah.
   Note: In Arabic.
               1965. June 29 (sample issue).

al-Ṭālib.
   Note: In Arabic.
               1978. Apr. 30 (sample issue).

Ṭarāblus al-Gharb. d.
   Note: In Arabic.
               1944–1951. Feb.–Dec. (microfilm).
               1954. Jan.-Oct. (microfilm).
               1961. Jan.–Nov. (microfilm).
               1967–1969. Jan.-Aug. (microfilm).

al-Thawrah.
   Note: In Arabic. Ceased publication Jan. 1972.
               1969–1972. Oct. 21–Jan. 10 (microfilm).

al-Yawm.
   Note: In Arabic.
               1968. May 25 (sample issue).

Madagascar

Antananarivo

Actuel. w., s-m., m., d. est. Oct. 12, 1979.
Note: Suspended publication Dec. 14, 1980–Mar. 1, Mar. 31–May, and
June–Aug. 1981. Ceased publication Nov. 25, 1981.
1979–1981. Oct. 12–Nov. 25 (microfilm).

Ady-gasy. s-w., w.
Note: In French and Malagasy. Ceased publication June 24, 1974.
1972–1974. June 27–June 24 (incomplete microfilm).

Ako takariva. t-w., w. est. Mar. 6, 1973.
Note: In French and Malagasy. Succeeds *Vatolahy*. Ceased publication
June 22, 1973.
1973. Apr. 28 (sample file).

Atrika. d. est. Dec. 1, 1976.
Note: In French and Malagasy.
1976. Dec. 1+ (microfilm).

Bas'y-vava. d.
Note: In Malagasy. Suspended publication May 3–21, 25–Sept. 27,
1974, Feb. 11–(July 1), 1975, Aug. 2, 1975–Feb. 6, 1976, Nov.
30, 1979–Feb. 9, 1980, and July 4, 1980–Dec. 17, 1982?
1973+ (microfilm).

Le Courrier de Madagascar. d. est. 1962?
Note: Ceased publication May 14, 1972. Succeeded by *Madagascar matin*,
May 29, 1972.
1962–1972. June 22–May 14 (microfilm).

La Démocratie populaire. m. est. Aug. 1981.
Note: In French and Malagasy.
1981. Aug. & Sept. (sample file).

Fandrosoana. w.
Note: In French and Malagasy. Ceased publication May 5, 1972.
1970–1972. Aug. 21–May 5 (microfilm).

France-Madagascar. d., w. est. 1942.
        1951–1952. Dec. 7–Dec. 31 (incomplete).
        1953 (fairly complete).
        1954. Jan. 4–Mar. 29, May 7–17.
        1956–1957. Feb. 29–Dec. 25 (incomplete).
        1958–1961.
        1962 (microfilm).

Gasikara vaovao. w. est. Aug. 17, 1973.
  Note: In Malagasy. Ceased publication Feb. 28, 1975.
        1973–1975. Aug. 17–Feb. 28 (microfilm).

Gazetin 'ny Malagasy. w.
  Note: In Malagasy.
        1952. July 23, Oct. 15–29, Nov. 26–Dec. 17.
        1953. Jan. 21–Feb. 4, 18–Apr. 8, Sept. 16, 23, Dec. 9, 16.
        1954. Jan. 6, 20–Feb. 3, May 12, 19.

Gazety roso. s-w. est. July 2, 1976.
  Note: In Malagasy.
        1976. July 2 (sample file).

Gazety ṣariaka. s-m.
  Note: In Malagasy. Ceased publication.
        1972. July 7 (sample file).

Hazolava. s-m. est. Aug. 28/Sept. 11, 1981.
  Note: In French and Malagasy. Suspended publication.
        1981. Aug. 28/Sept. 11 (sample file).

Hehy. d.
  Note: In French and Malagasy. Suspended publication Mar. 15–Apr.
        28, 1978. Ceased publication Jan. 13, 1979.
        1973–1979. Jan.–Jan. 13 (microfilm).

Imongo Vaovao. d.
  Note: In Malagasy.
        1961.
        1967+ (microfilm).

Isan' andro. d.
  Note: In French and Malagasy.
        1954. Jan. 19–23, 29–Feb. 6, May 29–Apr. 7, 10, 12, 13.

Le Journal de Madagascar. d., s-w.
        1952–1954 (incomplete).

Madagascar matin. est. May 29, 1972.
Note: In French and Malagasy. Succeeds *Le Courrier de Madagascar*.
1972. May 29+ (microfilm).

Madagasikara mahaleotena. d., s-w., w.
Note: In French and Malagasy. Suspended publication May 15–July 26,
1972. Ceased publication Sept. 5, 1973.
1968–1973. Jan.–Sept. 5 (microfilm).

Madagasikara-1947. w. est. Mar. 24, 1978.
Note: In Malagasy.
1981. Aug. 7 (sample file).

Madagasikara-rahampitso. w.
Note: In Malagasy.
1956. Mar. 1.

Mahiratra. t-w. est. Sept. 23, 1977.
Note: In Malagasy.
1980+

Malagasy mitolona. est. Mar. 4, 1977.
Note: In French and Malagasy.
1977. Mar. 4 (sample file).

Maresaka. d. est. 1954.
Note: In Malagasy. Suspended publication June 22–Dec. 23, 1977.
1971+ (microfilm).

Ny Gazety Malagasy. w. est. Feb. 3, 1981.
Note: In Malagasy.
1981. Feb. 3+

Ny marina. w.
Note: In Malagasy. Ceased publication Apr. 28, 1972.
1969–1972. Aug. 8–Apr. 21 (incomplete microfilm).

Ny Rariny ihany. w., d. est. June 7, 1974.
Note: In Malagasy. Suspended publication Feb. 7–Aug. 5, 1975.
Ceased publication Jan. 12, 1976.
1975. Feb. 7.
1975–1976. Aug. 5–Jan. 7.

Réalités malgaches. w. est. Jan. 29, 1982.
1982. Jan. 29+

Revolisiona Malagasy. w. est. Mar. 6, 1981.
Note: In Malagasy.
1981. Mar. 6, Oct. (sample file).

Sahy. d., s-w., w.
Note: In Malagasy. Suspended publication Aug. 21, 1978–Mar. 5,
1979.
1973+ (microfilm).

Sakaiza. est. Mar. 1, 1977.
Note: In Malagasy.
1977. Mar. 1 (sample file).

7 jours. w.
1956. Feb. 24.

Le Soir. d.
1956. Feb. 29.

Takariva isan' andro.
Note: In French and Malagasy.
1956. Mar. 2.

Tana-journal. w.
Note: In French.
1956. Feb. 24.

Telonohorefy. w.
Note: In Malagasy.
1976. Feb. 2/8 (sample file).

Tolom-bahoaka. w. est. June 4, 1982.
Note: In Malagasy. Succeeds *Vaovao* and *Fokonolona*.
1982. June 4+

La Tribune de Madagascar et dépendances. s-w.
1921. Apr. 8.

Tselatra. s-m.
Note: In French and Malagasy. Ceased publication May 11, 1973.
1973. Mar. 9.

Zavy misy. d. (irreg.) est. Sept. 8, 1972.
Note: In Malagasy. Title Sept. 8, 1972–Feb. 24, 1973, *Réalités malgaches*.
Ceased publication May 31, 1974.
1973–1974. Feb. 26–May 31 (microfilm).

Fianarantsoa

Lakroan'i Madagasikara. w.
  Note: In Malagasy.
              1971. July 11 (sample file).

Lumière. w.
  Note: Ceased publication Mar. 2, 1975.
              1956. Feb. 24.
              1968–1975. Jan.–Mar. 2 (microfilm).

Mahajanga

L'Aurore.w.
              1956. Feb. 18.

Kolo. s-m. est. May 14/28, 1982.
  Note: In French and Malagasy.
              1982. May 14/28 (sample file).
              1983. Jan. 28/Feb. 4.

Toamasina

Zava. w. est. Apr. 19, 1982.
  Note: In French.
              1982. Apr. 19 (sample file).

Malawi

Blantyre

Daily times. 5w.
  Note: Continues the *Times*.
       1973. Jan. 1+ (microfilm).

Malaŵi news. s-w., w. est. 1959.
  Note: In English and Chewa. Published in Limbe, 1961–1972.
       1961. May 18+ (microfilm).

The Times. w., s-w. est. 1895.
  Note: Established as the *Central African times*. Title (1943)–Oct. 4, 1963,
      Nyasaland times. Continued as the *Daily times*, Jan. 1, 1973.
       1943–1946 (microfilm).
       1947–1954.
       1955. Jan. 4–July 1, Nov. 11 (microfilm).
       1956. June 19–Dec. 28 (microfilm).
       1957–1960.
       1965–1972 (microfilm).

Mali

Bamako

L'Essor. d.
      1961+ (microfilm).

Le Soudan français. w.
  Note: Suspended publication (Nov. 10, 1955)–Oct. 15, 1956.
      1955. Sept. 29–Oct. 27.
      1956–1957. Oct. 15–June 29.

Mauritania

Nouakchott

Chaab. d.
  Note: In French.
          1977. July+ (microfilm).

Le Peuple. w.
          1971–1972. Aug. 13–Nov. 28 (microfilm).

al-Sha'b.
  Note: In Arabic.
          1971–1972. Oct. 15–Sept. 22 (incomplete microfilm).
          1978. Sept. + (microfilm).

Mauritius

Beau Bassin

Le Radical. w. est. 1981.
   Note: In French and English. Ceased publication.
      1981. Nov. 26/Dec. 2 (sample file).

Mont Lubin (Rodrigues)

L'Organisation. w. est. July 4, 1977.
      1978. June 26, July 4, 31, Aug. 7, 21, 28, Sept. 4, 11 (sample file).

Port Louis

Action. d. est. 1957.
      1964. May 11 (sample file).

Advance. d. est. 1940.
   Note: In English and French.
      1956–1961. Sept.-Dec. (fairly complete).
      1962+ (microfilm).

L'Aube. d. est. 1972.
   Note: Ceased publication Feb. 28, 1974?
      1973. Apr. 10.
      1974. Feb. 1–28 (microfilm).

Le Cernéen. d. except. Sunday. est. 1832.
   Note: In French and English. Ceased publication Feb. 2, 1981?
      1965. Nov. 3 (sample file).
      1979. Jan.-June (microfilm).

L'Express. d. est. 1963.
   Note: In French and English.
      1969+ (microfilm).

Horizons nouveaux. w. est. 1980.
   Note: In English and French.
      1982. June 20/27.

Hsin shang pao (New Chinese commercial paper). d. est. Mar. 8, 1956.
  Note: In Chinese.
            1970. Apr. 15, 16.
            1971. Mar. 22, July–Dec. (incomplete).
            1972–1975. Jan. 24–Nov. 19 (incomplete).

Le Journal du commerce et des affaires. w. est. 1981.
  Note: In French and English. Ceased publication.
            1981. Jan. 22/28, Mar. 31/Apr. 13, July 15/28 (sample file).

Lagazet lalit de klas. s-m. est. Aug. 7, 1981.
  Note: In French Creole of Mauritius.
            1981. Aug. 7 +

Le Mauricien. d. except Sunday. est. 1908.
  Note: In French and English.
            1966+ (microfilm).

Mauritius times. w. est. 1954.
  Note: In French and English.
            1979–1980. June 15–Dec. 7 (incomplete).
            1981. July 10/16 +

Le Militánt. d. est. Oct. 1, 1975.
  Note: Ceased publication May 9, 1978. Succeeded by *Le Peuple*.
            1977–1978. Jan. 1–May 9 (microfilm).

Nation. d. est. 1971.
  Note: In French and English.
            1971. May 5 (sample file).

Le Peuple. d. est. May 1978.
  Note: In French and English. Succeeds *Le Militant*. Ceased publication.
        Succeeded by *Le Nouveau militant*.
            1978–1979. May 26–June 23 (microfilm).

Le Populaire. d. est. 1973.
  Note: In French and English.
            1974. Mar. 14 (sample file).

Le Rassemblement. w. est. Aug. 1, 1980.
  Note: Ceased publication.
            1980–1981. Aug. 1–Mar. 16/23 (microfilm).

Star. d. est. 1963.
   Note: In French and English. Ceased publication Sept. 17, 1979.
             1970. Sept. 28 (sample file).
             1974-1979. Jan.-Sept. 27 (microfilm).

Sunday nation.
   Note: In French and English.
             1981. Jan. 11 (sample file).

Sunday star. est. Jan. 6, 1980.
   Note: In French and English.
             1980-1981. Jan. 6-Aug. 30 (incomplete microfilm).

Port Mathurin (Rodrigues)

Le Rodriguais. w. est. Dec. 23, 1980.
   Note: Suspended publication Dec. 11, 1982?-June 3, 1983?
             1980-1981. Dec. 23-Dec. 23 (microfilm).
             1982. Jan. 22-Dec. 11 (incomplete).

Quatre Bornes

The Hindu. w. est. Mar. 6, 1981.
   Note: In English and French.
             1981. Mar. 6 (sample file).

Morocco

Casablanca

al-'Adālah.
  Note: In Arabic.
    1977. Jan. 21 (sample issue).

al-Ahdāf.
  Note: In Arabic.
    1965. Mar. 20 (sample issue).

Atlantic courier. d. est. July 1, 1952.
  Note: Succeeds *Maroc presse*; American edition. Ceased publication Sept.
    12, 1952. Succeeded by *Moroccan courier*.
    1952. July 2–Sept. 12.

al-Bayān. d.
  Note: In Arabic.
    1973. Sept. 21+ (microfilm).

al Bayane. d. est. 1972.
  Note: In French.
    1973. Jan. 10 (sample file).
    1977. July+. (microfilm).

Filasṭin.
  Note: In Arabic.
    1970. Jan. 9 (sample issue).

al-Ittiḥād al-waṭanī.
  Note: In Arabic.
    1973. Apr. 19 (sample issue).

al-Kifāḥ al-waṭanī.
  Note: In Arabic.
    1965. May 28 (sample issue).

Maghreb informations. d. est. 1966.
    1966. July 26 (sample file).

Maroc demain. w.
    1953–1955. Dec. 26–Feb. 12 (microfilm).
    1956–1973. May 5–Oct. (microfilm).

Maroc informations. d.
>   1966. Mar. 31 (sample file).

Maroc-presse. d.
>   Note: Succeeds *La Presse marocaine-Le Maroc quotidien* sometime between July 28, 1949 and Feb. 25, 1950. Ceased publication Apr. 30, 1956.
>   >   1950. Feb. 25–Dec. 31.
>   >   1951–1952 (incomplete).
>   >   1953.
>   >   1954. Jan.–Apr., Oct. 22(m).
>   >   1955–1956. June 17–Apr. 30 (fairly complete).

Maroc-presse; American edition. d. est. Sept. 15, 1951.
>   Note: In English. Ceased publication June 30, 1952. Succeeded by *Atlantic courier.*
>   >   1951. Sept. 15, Oct. 13.
>   >   1952. Jan. 17–June 30.

Maroc-soir. d. est. Nov. 1, 1971.
>   Note: Succeeds *La Vigie marocaine.*
>   >   1971–1972. Nov.–Dec.
>   >   1973+ (microfilm).

al-Masīrah al-khaḍrā'.
>   Note: In Arabic.
>   >   1976. Oct. 16 (sample issue).

Mediterranean courier. w. est. Apr. 11, 1958.
>   1958–1959. Apr. 11–July 23 (incomplete).

Moroccan courier. w. est. Oct. 20, 1952.
>   Note: Succeeds *Atlantic courier.* Removed from Tangier.
>   >   1952. Oct. 20.
>   >   1953–1954. Apr. 18–Dec. 31.
>   >   1955–1958. Jan. 7–Apr. 4 (incomplete).

al-Muḥarrir.
>   Note: In Arabic.
>   >   1977 (microfilm).

al-Niḍāl.
>   Note: In Arabic.
>   >   1973. Apr. 30 (sample issue).

Le Petit marocain; le progres marocain. d. est.1912.
  Note: Ceased publication Nov. 1, 1971. Succeeded by *Le Matin*.
        1940. Apr. 21(m), Oct. 11, Nov. 9, Dec. 17.
        1941-1946. Jan. 31-Apr. 26 (incomplete).
        1951-1952. Jan. 1-Nov. 4.
        1954-1956. Jan.-Aug.
        1956. Sept. 1-5, Oct. 30.
        1959.
        1960-1961 (fairly complete).
        1962-1971. Jan.-Nov. 1 (microfilm).

La Presse marocaine. d. est. 1913.
  Note: Incorporated *Le Soir marocain*. Merged with *Le Maroc quotidien*
        sometime between June 21-July 15, 1949, to form *Le Maroc quoti-
        dien-la presse marocaine*.
        1942. Nov. 8-Dec. 27 (incomplete).
        1943-1945. Feb. 3-Oct. 23.
        1946. Mar. 1-May 4 (incomplete).
        1946-1947. Sept. 30-Dec.
        1948-1949. Jan.-June 21 (incomplete).

La Presse marocaine: le Maroc quotidien. d. est. 1949.
  Note: Title until sometime between July 15-18, 1949, *Le Maroc quotidien-
        la presse marocaine*, formed sometime between June 21-July 15,
        1949, by the merger of *Le Maroc quotidien* and *La Presse marocaine*.
        Succeeded by *Maroc-presse* sometime between July 28, 1949 and
        Feb. 25, 1950.
        1949. July 15, 18.

al-Taḥrīr. d.
  Note: In Arabic.
        1961. Jan. 13-Dec. 30 (microfilm).

al-'Ummāl.
  Note: In Arabic.
        1962. May 2 (sample issue).

La Vigie marocaine. d. est. 1907?
  Note: Ceased publication Oct. 31, 1971. Succeeded by *Maroc-soir*.
        1940-1941. Oct.-Dec. (incomplete).
        1942-1944.
        1945-1946 (incomplete).
        1947 (fairly complete).
        1948-1949 (incomplete).
        1950. Jan. 14, 21, 24, Mar.-Dec.
        1951-1956.
        1957-1971. Jan.-Oct. (microfilm).

Ceuta

El Faro. d. est. 1934.
  Note: In Spanish.
              1939. Sept. 15.
              1942. Nov.-Dec. (incomplete).
              1943-1944. Jan.-June.
              1944-1945. July 20-Nov. 11 (fairly complete).

Fez

Le Courrier du Maroc. d. est. 1929.
  Note: Ceased publication Apr. 1962?
              1941-1942. Dec. 15-Jan. 15.
              1942-1945. July-Dec. (fairly complete).
              1946. Jan. 4-Apr. 17, Nov. 28-Dec. 31 (incomplete).
              1947-1951. Jan. 2-Apr. 20.
              1951-1954. Nov. 15-Dec.
              1955-1957. Jan.-Sept. 13 (fairly complete).
              1958. Dec. 5, 7, 11, 13-17, 20-31.
              1959. Jan.-Nov. (fairly complete).
              1960-1961. Aug. 5-Jan. 6 (fairly complete).

Fās.
  Note: In Arabic.
              1971. June (sample issue).

Meknes

Hādhihi al-dunyā.
  Note: In Arabic.
              1965. June 1 (sample issue).

Melilla

El Telegrama del Rif. d.
  Note: In Spanish.
              1950. May 4-June 1, Aug. 13, Sept. 1-3, 6-16, 19-Oct. 31.
              1952.

Rabat

Āfāq siyāsīyah.
  Note: In Arabic.
              1973. Apr. 16 (sample issue).

al-Akhbār.
    Note: In Arabic.
          1973. Apr. 16 (sample issue).

al-'Alam. d. est. 1946.
    Note: In Arabic.
          1946-1952. Sept. 16-Dec. (microfilm).
          1956. Jan.-June (microfilm).
          1961 (microfilm).
          1967 (microfilm).
          1971+ (microfilm).

al-Anbā'. d.
    Note: In Arabic.
          1976. Nov.+ (microfilm).

Aṣdā'.
    Note: In Arabic.
          Current issues held for one year only.

al-Barlamān.
    Note: In Arabic.
          1970. Jan. 5 (sample issue).

L'Echo du Maroc. d. est. 1912.
    Note: Ceased publication May 8, 1962.
          1942. Nov. 8-10, 13-18.
          1943-1954.
          1959-1960. Feb. 7-Apr. 30.

al-Faḍā'ih.
    Note: In Arabic.
          1965. May 31 (sample issue).

al-Fallāh.
    Note: In Arabic.
          1970. Jan. 9 (sample issue).

al-Ḥarakah.
    Note: In Arabic.
          1978-1979. Mar. 21-Mar. 21 (incomplete).

al-Ḥurrīyah.
    Note: In Arabic.
          1978. Aug. 31 (sample issue).

al-Ithnayn.
  Note: In Arabic.
         1977–1978. Oct. 14–Nov. 6.

al-Janūb.
  Note: In Arabic.
         1963. Oct. 4 (sample issue).

al-Kawālīs.
  Note: In Arabic.
         1972. Jan. 25 (sample issue).

al-Maghrib. d. est. Oct. 17, 1977.
  Note: In French.
         1977–1978. Oct. 17–Dec. (microfilm).
         1979. Jan. & Mar. (microfilm).
         1982. Feb. +

al-Maghrib al-'Arabī.
  Note: In Arabic.
         1978. Apr. 28 (sample issue).

al-Ma'rakah.
  Note: In Arabic.
         1965. May/June (sample issue).

Le Matin du Sahara. est. Nov. 1, 1971.
  Note: Succeeds *Le Petit marocain*. Title Nov. 1, 1971 until sometime be-
         fore Nov. 23, 1975, *Le Matin*.
         1973. Oct.–Dec. (microfilm).
         1977. Mar. + (microfilm).

al-Mīthāq al-waṭanī.
  Note: In Arabic.
         1977–1979. Sept. 2–Mar. 31.

al-Muḥarrir.
  Note: In Arabic.
         1977+ (microfilm).

al-Niḍāl.
  Note: In Arabic.
         1965. May 29 (sample issue).

L'Opinion. d. est. 1965.
         1966. July+ (incomplete microfilm).

Risālat al-Maghrib.
　　Note: In Arabic.
　　　　　1947–1952. Aug. 1–Nov. 18 (microfilm).

al-Sa'ādah.
　　Note: In Arabic.
　　　　　1941–1942. Mar. 18–Apr. 9 (microfilm).
　　　　　1942–1943. June 10–Dec. 30 (incomplete microfilm).

Saḥrā'unā.
　　Note: In Arabic.
　　　　　1967. Sept. 22 (sample issue).

Ṣawt al-Maghrib.
　　Note: In Arabic.
　　　　　1963. Jan. 19 (sample issue).

Ṣawt al-ṭālib/La Voix de l'étudiant.
　　Note: In Arabic.
　　　　　1972. Oct. 24 (sample issue).

al-Sha'b.
　　Note: In Arabic.
　　　　　1964. Mar. 30 (sample issue).

al-Shabāb.
　　Note: In Arabic.
　　　　　1958. Aug. 23 (sample issue).

al-Ṣiḥāfah.
　　Note: In Arabic.
　　　　　1973. Apr. 28 (sample issue).

al-Usbū'.
　　Note: In Arabic.
　　　　　1965. June 28 (sample issue).

La Vie economique. w. est. 1921.
　　　　　1972. Mar. 10 (sample issue).

al-Waṭan.
　　Note: In Arabic.
　　　　　1965. Apr. 21 (sample issue).

Tangier

La Dépêche marocaine. d. est. Dec. 15, 1905.
      1942. Dec. 17, 19.
      1943–1948. Jan.–Sept.
      1949–1954. Jan. 1–Nov. 9 (fairly complete).
      1955–1957. Feb. 28–May 16 (incomplete).

L'Echo de Tanger et de la Méditerranée. w. est. 1925.
      1942. Dec. 6, 27.
      1943. Mar. 28, May 2, 9, 30, June 6, 27, July 18.
      1943–1944. Aug. 1–May 21.

España. d. est. 1938.
  Note: In Spanish.
      1939. Nov. 23.
      1941. Apr. 28–Dec. 11 (incomplete).
      1942. Apr. 17–Dec. (incomplete).
      1943–1948.
      1949. Jan. 4–Aug. 31 (incomplete).
      1950. Apr.–May, Sept.–Oct.
      1952–1953.
      1954. Jan. 2–6, Apr. 23–Nov. 9.
      1955. June 28–Oct. 29 (incomplete).
      1956. Feb. 20–Dec. 27 (incomplete).

Le Journal de Tanger. w. est. 1905.
  Note: In French, English, Spanish and Arabic.
      1943–1944. Aug. 5–Dec. 24.

Tangier gazette and Morocco mail. French edition. d.
  Note: Ceased publication Mar. 31, 1945.
      1941–1945. Nov. 17–Mar. (incomplete).

Tangier gazette and Morocco mail. Spanish edition. d.
  Note: Ceased publication Sept. 3, 1945.
      1941–1943. Nov. 17–Dec. (incomplete).
      1944.
      1945. Jan.–Mar.

Tangier gazette and times of Morocco. s-w., w. est. 1883.
> Note: Title until Sept. 2, 1955, *Tangier gazette and Morocco mail.* Ceased
> publication Aug. 27, 1960?
>> 1941-1943. Nov. 21-Dec. (fairly complete).
>> 1944-1948.
>> 1949 (fairly complete).
>> 1950-1956.
>> 1957. May 17-June 7, 21, Aug. 23.
>> 1960. Feb. 26-July 8 (incomplete).

Times of Morocco. m., w. est. July 5, 1884.
> Note: Suspended publication July 9, 1885-Jan. 16, 1886.
>> 1884-1885. July 5-July 9.
>> 1886-1889. Jan. 16-July 12.

La Tribune de Tanger. w. est. Apr. 1950.
>> 1954. Oct. 11.

Tetuan

El Día. d.
> Note: In Spanish and Arabic.
>> 1951-1954. Dec. 17-Nov. 9 (incomplete).
>> 1955. Dec. 4-31.
>> 1956. Jan.-June, July 11-Aug. 28, Dec. 11-26.
>> 1957. Feb. 11-Apr. 30, Sept. 2-Nov. 30.

Diario de Africa. d. est. Dec. 1, 1945.
> Note: In Spanish.
>> 1945-1948. Dec.-Dec.
>> 1949. Mar. 1-Apr. 27, June, Aug. 2, 6, 9-31.
>> 1950. May 5-June 17, Sept.-Oct. (fairly complete).
>> 1951. Aug., Oct., Dec. (incomplete).
>> 1952-1953. Jan.-Apr. (incomplete).
>> 1954. Apr. 21-Dec. 9 (incomplete).
>> 1955-1956. May 1-Nov. 8 (incomplete).
>> 1967. Feb. 3 (sample file).

Marruecos. d.
> Note: In Spanish.
>> 1942. Oct. 3.
>> 1943. Jan. 15-July 31 (incomplete).
>> 1943-1945. Aug.-Nov.

al-Mawqif al-usbū'ī.
> Note: In Arabic.
>> 1965. May 23 (sample issue).

Mozambique

Beira

Beira news. s-w.
　　Note: In English and Portuguese.
　　　　　1943. Mar. 18, 22.

Diário de Moçambique. d. est. 1950.
　　Note: Ceased publication Mar. 15, 1971.
　　　　　1955. Oct. 16.
　　　　　1961 (fairly complete).
　　　　　1962-1971. Jan.-Mar. 15 (microfilm).

Diário de Moçambique. d. est. Sept. 25, 1981.
　　Note: Succeeds *Notícias da Beira*.
　　　　　1981. Sept. 25+ (microfilm).

Notícias da Beira. b-w., d. est. 1915.
　　Note: Ceased publication Sept. 16, 1981. Succeeded by *Diário de Moçam-
　　　　bique*.
　　　　　1955. Jan. 7.
　　　　　1971-1981. Mar. 16-Sept. 16 (microfilm).

Voz africana. w.
　　　　　1963-1966 (microfilm).
　　　　　1972-1974. Jan.-Aug. (incomplete microfilm).

Maputo

O Brado africano. w.
　　Note: In Portuguese and Ronga.
　　　　　1942. Nov. 14(m).
　　　　　1943. Feb. 6(m), May 15(m)-29(m), July 10(m).

Combate. w. est. Sept. 25, 1981.
　　　　　1981. Sept. 25+

Diário. d. est. 1956.
　　Note: Succeeds the *Lourenço Marques guardian*. Ceased publication in 1974
　　　　or 1975.
　　　　　1960. Nov. 16-Dec. 31.
　　　　　1963-1974. Jan.-Apr. (microfilm).

Lourenço Marques guardian. t-w., d. est. 1905.
    Note: In English and Portuguese. Succeeded by *Diário* in 1956.
                1944-1945. Feb. 10-Dec. 29 (incomplete).
                1946. Feb. 6-21, 26-Mar. 12, Apr.-Dec.
                1947-1948. Jan.-Aug.
                1948-1949. Sept.-Dec. (fairly complete).
                1950 (incomplete).
                1951. Aug. 29, Dec. 19.
                1952. Jan. 1-Feb. 15, July 16-Dec. 30 (incomplete).
                1953.

Notícias. d. est. 1926.
                1945-1952. Apr. 14-May 6.
                1954. Jan. 10-Dec. 28 (fairly complete).
                1955. Feb.-Dec.
                1956+ (microfilm).

A Tribuna. d. except Sun. est. 1962.
    Note: Ceased publication in 1974 or 1975.
                1965. Oct. 12 (sample file).

União. w.
                1953. Apr. 27.

Namibia

Windhoek

Allgemeine Zeitung. 5w. est. 1915.
  Note: In German.
            1955–1956. Dec. 15–June 30.
            1956. July–Dec. (fairly complete).
            1957–1958.
            1959–1965 (microfilm).
            1972+ (microfilm).

Joernaal.
  Note: In Afrikaans.
            1980. May 16 (sample file).

Die Republikein. t-w., d. est. Dec. 1, 1977.
  Note: In Afrikaans.
            1977. Dec. 1+ (microfilm).

Die Süidwes-Afrikaner. w., s-w. est. 1928.
  Note: In Afrikaans.
            1952–1954. July–Dec. (fairly complete).
            1962–1963. Nov. 13–Dec. 31 (incomplete microfilm).

Die Süidwester. w., s-w., 5w. est. 1945.
  Note: In Afrikaans.
            1952–1953. Jan. 23–Dec. 19 (incomplete).
            1976–1977. Nov. 6–Dec. 31 (microfilm).

Windhoek advertiser. s-w., 5w. est. July 4, 1919.
            1943–1944.
            1945–1951 (fairly complete).
            1952–1953.
            1955–1956. Sept. 9–Dec. 28.
            1962+ (microfilm).

Windhoek observer. d. est. 1978.
            1979. Aug. 18 (sample file).

Niger

Niamey

Le Sahel. d. est. Apr. 29, 1974.
        1974. Apr. 29+ (microfilm).

Sahel hebdo. est. May 20, 1974.
        1974. May 20+ (microfilm).

Nigeria

Aba

Eastern states express. d. est. 1949.
    1963–1965. July–June (microfilm).

Apapa

Morning post. est. Oct. 1, 1961.
  Note: Title Oct. 1–(Dec. 22), 1961, *Nigerian morning post*. Ceased publication Jan. 1973?
    1961. Oct. 1, 2, 7, 12, Dec. 6–8, 22.
    1962–1973. Jan.–Jan. 25 (incomplete microfilm).

Benin

Nigerian observer. d. est. May 29, 1968.
    1971. Aug. 5+ (microfilm).

Calabar

Nigerian chronicle. w., d. est. 1971.
    1974+ (microfilm).

Nigerian weekly record. est. 1935.
  Note: Title until July 7, 1951, *Nigerian eastern mail*. Ceased publication Sept. 15, 1951. Succeeded by *Nigerian daily record*, Enugu.
    1943–1949. July 24–Dec.
    1950–1951. Jan. 7–June 23 (incomplete).
    1951. July 7–21, Aug. 4–Sept. 8.

Enugu

Daily star.
  Note: Continues *Renaissance*, Oct. 1, 1975.
    1975. Oct. 1+ (microfilm).

Eastern sentinel. d. est. 1955.
  Note: Ceased publication Aug. 31, 1961.
    1956. Feb. 6.

Nigerian daily record. est. Oct. 15, 1951.
   Note: Succeeds *Nigerian weekly record*, Calabar. Ceased publication Mar.
      31, 1952.
         1951-1952. Oct. 15-Mar. 31.

Nigerian outlook. w., d. est. May 3, 1951.
   Note: Title May 1951-Oct. 28, 1954, *Eastern outlook and Cameroons star*,
      Nov. 4, 1954 until Sept. 1, 1960, *Eastern outlook*. Ceased publica-
      tion May 29, 1967.
         1951-1955. July 5-Dec. 29 (fairly complete).
         1956-1957. Jan. 5-Dec. 12 (incomplete).
         1958-1960. Jan. 2-Aug. 18.
         1960-1961. Nov. 8-Dec.
         1962-1966. Jan.-Mar. 7 (microfilm).

Renaissance. w., d. est. Oct. 1, 1970.
   Note: Continued by the *Daily star*, Oct. 1, 1975.
         1970-1975. Oct.-Sept. (microfilm).

Ibadan

Daily sketch. est. 1964.
   Note:· Title [Dec. 2, 1964], *Nigerian daily sketch*.
         1964. Dec. 2 (sample file).
         1978. July+ (microfilm).

Gboungboun. w.
   Note: In Yoruba.
         1979. Oct. 10/16, 24/30, 31/Nov. 6.
         1982. Mar. 31/Apr. 6+

Irohin Yoruba. w. est. 1945.
         1963-1966. Mar.-Dec. (incomplete microfilm).
         1973. Aug.+ (microfilm).

Nigerian tribune. d. est. 1949.
         1952. Feb. 11-Dec. 31 (incomplete).
         1953-1955.
         1956-1959 (incomplete).
         1960.
         1961-1964 (microfilm).
         1971. July+ (microfilm).

Southern Nigeria defender. d. est. 1943.
Note: Published in Warri until July 16, 1945; Lagos, Aug. 2–15, 1945;
          Ibadan from Nov. 13, 1945.
                1944–1945. July–June (incomplete).
                1945. Aug. 2–15, Nov. 13–Dec. 31 (incomplete).
                1946–1947. Jan. 2–Oct. 23 (fairly complete).

Ikeja

Amana. w.
Note: In Hausa.
                1981. Apr. 6–Aug. 31 (incomplete microfilm).

Financial punch. w. est. 1981.
                1981. Feb. 9 (sample file).
                1981. July 6–Sept. 7 (incomplete).
                1982. Oct. 27/Nov. 3.

National concord. d. est. Mar. 2, 1980.
                1980. Mar. 2+ (microfilm).

Punch. d. est. 1976.
                1978. Aug.+ (microfilm).

Sunday people.
                1979. Aug. 5 (sample file).

Ilorin

Nigerian herald. d. est. 1973.
                1975+ (microfilm).

Jos

Middle Belt herald.
                1965. June 1 (sample file).

Nigeria standard. w., d.
                1974 + (microfilm).

'Yancin dan adam. w.
Note: In Hausa.
                1981. Apr.–Aug. 26 (microfilm).

Kaduna

Gaskiya ta fi Kwabo. s-w. est. 1939.
  Note: In Hausa. Removed from Zaria sometime after Aug. 14, 1964.
      1973 + (microfilm).

New Nigerian. d. est. Jan. 1, 1966.
  Note: Succeeds the *Nigerian citizen*, Zaria.
      1966 + (microfilm).

Kano

Daily comet. est. 1931.
  Note: In English and Hausa. Ceased publication June 15, 1966.
      1962-1966. Mar. 29-May 24 (incomplete microfilm).

Daily mail. est. Mar. 1, 1961.
  Note: Ceased publication June 27, 1964.
      1961. Mar.-Dec.
      1962-1964. Jan.-May (microfilm).

Northern star. d. est. 1958.
      1962-1965. Dec.-Dec. (incomplete microfilm).

Lagos

Business times. w.
      1980. Dec. 2 +

Daily comet. est. May 16, 1944.
  Note: Title until Nov. 3 or 4, 1944, *Comet*.
      1944. May 19, 20, June 5, Nov. 25, 28.
      1945. Apr. 9-14.
      1946. May-Dec. (incomplete).
      1947.

Daily express. est. Sept. 19, 1960.
  Note: Succeeds *Daily service*. Suspended publication Nov. 23, 1965-Aug.
      1, 1969. Ceased publication 1975?
      1960-1965. Sept. 19-Aug. (microfilm).
      1972-1975. Sept.-Feb. (microfilm).

Daily service. est. June 27, 1938.
   Note: Ceased publication Sept. 17, 1960. Succeeded by *Daily express.*
          1942-1955. Nov. 2-Dec. (incomplete microfilm).
          1956. Sept.-Dec. (incomplete microfilm).
          1957-1958. Jan.-Aug. (microfilm).
          1959. Apr.-June (microfilm).
          1959-1960. Nov.-Sept. 17 (microfilm).

Daily telegraph. est. July 4, 1958.
   Note: Ceased publication Feb. 23, 1967.
          1964. Sept. 24 (sample file).

Daily times. est. 1925.
   Note: Title until Jan. 3, 1949, *Nigerian daily times.*
          1930. Feb. 4-Aug. 30.
          1942. June 26, 27.
          1944. May 10-Nov. 4 (incomplete).
          1945. Jan. 16, Mar. 10, 13.
          1946-1948. Jan. 28-Dec. 31.
          1949. Jan. 4-Sept. 30, Nov.-Dec. (fairly complete).
          1950-1951.
          1952. Jan.-Oct., Dec.
          1953-1955. Jan.-Aug. (fairly complete).
          1956 + (microfilm).

Nationalist. w. est. 1978.
          1978-1979. Dec. 10-Dec. 16/22 (incomplete).

Nigerian mercantile guardian. w. est. Oct. 31, 1951.
   Note: Ceased publication Oct. 6, 1956.
          1953. Apr. 25.

Nigerian statesman. w. est. July 5, 1947.
   Note: Ceased publication Feb. 15, 1958.
          1947. July 5-Sept. 20.

Sunday express. est. Oct. 4, 1959.
   Note: Ceased publication Nov. 21, 1965.
          1965. Oct. 17 (sample file).

Sunday post. est. Aug. 13, 1961.
          1961. Aug. 13-Oct. 15, Nov. 5-Dec. 31.
          1962-1964 (incomplete microfilm).

Sunday times. est. Aug. 2, 1953.
>> 1963–1965. Jan.–June (incomplete microfilm).

Truth. w.
>> 1953. Apr. 24.

Weekly focus.
>> 1979. Nov. 19 (sample file).

Maiduguri

Albishir. w.
> Note: In English.
>> 1975. Nov. 29.

Makurdi

The Nigeria voice. d. est. 1981.
>> 1982. Nov. 18 (sample file).

Onitsha

Eastern observer. d. except Sunday. est. Jan. 8, 1959.
> Note: In English and Ibo. Ceased publication Dec. 31, 1965.
>> 1963. May–Dec. (microfilm).
>> 1964. Feb. 3–Apr. 30 (microfilm).

Nigerian mirror. d.
>> 1975 (microfilm).

Nigerian spokesman. d. est. Mar. 1, 1943.
> Note: Ceased publication May 20, 1967.
>> 1943–1944. Mar.–June (incomplete).
>> 1944. Dec. 2–9.
>> 1945 (incomplete).
>> 1946 (fairly complete).
>> 1947.
>> 1948. Jan. 2–May 14 (incomplete).

Owerri

Nigerian statesman. d. est. June 11, 1979?
>> 1979. July + (microfilm).

Port Harcourt

Eastern Nigeria guardian. d. est. 1940.
  Note: Ceased publication May 30, 1967.
        1944. Feb. 21–25, Aug.–Dec.
        1945 (incomplete).
        1946–1948. Jan. 2–May 25.

Nigerian observer. s-w. est. 1930.
  Note: Ceased publication Dec. 17, 1960.
        1955. Sept. 9.

Nigerian tide. w., d. est. Dec. 4, 1971.
        1971. Dec. 4, 11 (microfilm).
        1972. Feb. 12 (microfilm).
        1973. Nov. 17 + (microfilm).

Yaba

Advance. w. est. Aug. 16, 1965.
        1967–1976. Oct. 8/14–Apr. 10 (incomplete microfilm).

West African pilot. d. est. Nov. 22, 1937.
        1937–1939. Nov. 22–Nov. 11 (incomplete microfilm).
        1941–1977. Apr. 7–Dec. (microfilm).

Zaria

Albishir. s-w. est. Oct. 26, 1951.
  Note: In the vernacular. Ceased publication June 1960.
        1953. Mar. 28.

Bornu people. d.
  Note: In English, Hausa and Kanuri.
        1963–1964. Mar. 23–July 18 (incomplete microfilm).

Gaskiya ta fi Kwabo. w., s-w. est. 1939.
  Note: In Hausa. Removed to Kaduna sometime after Aug. 14, 1964 and
        before Feb. 4, 1974.
        1944–1950. Jan. 5–Nov. 29 (fairly complete).
        1951–1952. Sept. 26–Dec. 17 (fairly complete).
        1953–1955. Jan. 7–May 11.
        1962–1964. Dec. 14–Aug. 14 (incomplete microfilm).

Jakadiya. fortnightly. est. 1946.
Note: In Hausa. Ceased publication Nov. 1965.
1953. Mar. 16.

Mwanger u Tiv. w.
Note: In the vernacular. Ceased publication July 1960.
1953. May 25.

Nigerian citizen. w., s-w. est. 1948.
Note: Ceased publication Dec. 29, 1965. Succeeded by *New Nigerian*, Kaduna.
1950-1951. Oct. 27-Mar. 16 (fairly complete).
1953-1954. Apr. 30-June 24 (incomplete).
1958-1961. Jan. 25-Dec. 30.
1962. Jan. 3, 6.
1962-1965. Oct. 27-Dec. 29 (microfilm).

Sodangi kano.
Note: In Hausa.
1953. Apr. 13.

Réunion

Saint-Denis

Croix sud.
         1972. Mar. 5 (sample file).

La Démocratie. t-w.
         1965. Sept. 16 (sample file).

Fanal. w. est. Sept. 1981.
    Note: Oct. 2, 1981 is number 1. Ceased publication Nov. 14, 1981?
         1981. Sept., Oct. 2 (sample file).

L'Hebdo.
         1979. Oct. 17 (sample file).

Le Journal de l'Île de la Réunion. d. est. 1950?
         1963 + (microfilm).

Le Peuple. d. est. 1908.
         1956–1957.
         1958. Jan. 7–May 6.

Le Progrès. w.
         1965. Feb. 21 (sample file).

Le Quotidien de la Réunion et de l'Ocean Indien. d. est. 1976.
         1976. Oct. + (microfilm).

Témoignage chrétien de la Réunion. s-m. est. 1971?
    Note: Ceased publication Oct. 15/31, 1981.
         1975–1981. May–Oct. (microfilm).

Témoignages. d. est. 1944.
         1967. Jan. 18 + (microfilm).

Saint-Joseph

Action Réunionnaise. w.
         1973. Oct. (sample file).

Rwanda

Kigali

Kinyamateka. s-m. est. 1933.
   Note: In Rwanda. Removed from Kabgayi during 1972.
      1968 + (microfilm).

La Relève. w., s-m. est. Jan. 12/18, 1976.
   Note: Absorbed *Rwanda Carrefour d'Afrique.*
      1976. Jan. 12/18 + (microfilm).

São Tomé and Principe

São Tomé

A Voz S. Tomé. w.
        1970 (incomplete microfilm).
        1972–1974. June–Apr. (microfilm).

Senegal

Dakar

Dakar-Matin. w., s-w., t-w., d. est. Feb. 3, 1933.
  Note: Title until Apr. 5, 1961, *Paris-Dakar*. Ceased publication May 16,
      1970. Succeeded by *Le Soleil*.
          1933-1934. Jan. 31 (Spec. #), Feb. 8-Dec. 25 (microfilm).
          1941-1944. Nov.-Dec.
          1948-1949. Sept.-Dec. (incomplete).
          1950-1953.
          1954. Jan.-Apr., July-Dec.
          1955. Jan., July-Dec.
          1956. Jan.-Aug. (fairly complete).
          1958. Aug.-Dec. (incomplete).
          1959-1970. Jan.-May 16 (microfilm).

Le Soleil. d. est. May 20, 1970.
  Note: Succeeds *Dakar-Matin*.
          1970. May 20 + (microfilm).

Vérité. m?
          1979. Jan. (sample file).

Seychelles

Victoria

L'Écho des Îles. s-m. est. Jan. 15, 1980.
  Note: In French and Creole.
          1980. Jan. 15.
          1983. Jan. 15.

Nation. d. est. June 29, 1976.
  Note: In English, French and Creole. Succeeds the *Seychelles bulletin*.
          Ceased publication June 4, 1977. Succeeded by the *Nation*, estab-
          lished June 9, 1977.
          1976-1977. June 29-June 4 (microfilm).

Nation. d. est. June 9, 1977.
  Note: In English, French and Creole. Succeeds the *Nation*, which ceased
          publication June 4, 1977.
          1977. June 10 + (microfilm).

People. m., irreg. est. Dec. 23, 1975.
  Note:In English, French or Creole. Suspended publication July 1977-
          Mar. 1978, and [Apr. 1978?]-Nov. 9, 1979.
          1975. Dec. 23 + (microfilm).

Le Seychellois. s-w., d. est. 1903.
  Note: In French and English. Ceased publication Nov. 9, 1977?
          1956-1959. Oct. 10-Dec. 30 (incomplete).
          1960.
          1961-1977. Jan.-Nov. 9 (microfilm).

Sierra Leone

Daily mail. est. 1931.
   Note: Title until July 31, 1952, *Sierra Leone daily mail*. Incorporated the
      Sierra Leone weekly news sometime between Nov. 1951 and Apr.
      1953.
         1952–1955. Nov.–Dec. (microfilm).
         1961.
         1962 + (microfilm).

Nation. d. est. 1971.
         1975. Nov. 1, 3.

People. irreg. est. June 2, 1972.
   Note: Ceased publication Apr. 14, 1973?
         1972–1973. June 2–Apr. 14 (microfilm).

Sierra Leone guardian. w. est. 1906.
         1926. Apr. 23, 30.

Sierra Leone weekly news. est. Sept. 6, 1884.
   Note: Ceased publication sometime between Nov. 1951 and Apr. 1953.
      Incorporated by the *Daily mail*.
         1889. Nov. 16.
         1926. Apr. 24.
         1943–1944 (incomplete).
         1945.
         1946 (fairly complete).
         1947–1948.
         1949–1950 (fairly complete).
         1951. Aug. 11–25, Sept. 29/Oct. 6, 13/20, Nov. 3/10.

Sierra Leonean. w. est. Feb. 2, 1961.
         1965–1967. Jan.–June (microfilm).

Unity.
         1967. Sept. 15, 25, Oct. 6 (sample file).

We Yone. w., s-w.
   Note: In English.
         1973 (microfilm).
         1978 + (microfilm).

Somalia

Hargeisa

Somaliland news. b-w., w. est. Nov. 20, 1958.
  Note: In English and Arabic. Succeeds *War Somali Sidihi.* Ceased publication Dec. 12, 1960. Succeeded by *Somali news,* Mogadishu, Mar. 31, 1961.
    1958–1960. Dec. 22–Aug. 22 (incomplete microfilm).

War Somali Sidihi. fortnightly. est. Jan. 17, 1953.
  Note: Ceased publication Nov. 1, 1958. Succeeded by *Somaliland news.*
    1956–1958. Nov. 17–Nov. 1 (microfilm).

Mogadishu

Il Corriere della Somalia. d.
  Note: In Italian and Arabic. Succeeds the *Somalia courier; Corriere della Somalia* sometime between Mar. 29 and May 18, 1950. Ceased publication Oct. 22, 1969. Succeeded by *Stella d'Ottobre.*
    1950. May 18–July 28 (incomplete).
    1951–1955. Jan. 23–Dec. 30 (incomplete).
    1956 (fairly complete).
    1957–1958. Apr. 4–June 9 (incomplete).
    1960–1961. Oct.–Dec.
    1964–1969. Jan.–Oct. 22 (microfilm).

Dawn. w. est. Nov. 14, 1969.
  Note: Ceased publication Jan. 19, 1973.
    1969–1973. Nov. 14–Jan. 19 (microfilm).

al-Fajr.
  Note: In Arabic.
    1969–1970. Nov. 21–Jan. 30 (microfilm).

Heegan. w. est. July 17, 1978.
  Note: In English.
    1978. July 17 + (microfilm).

Najmat Uktūbar. d. est. Oct. 23, 1969.
  Note: In Arabic. Succeeds *Sawt al-Ṣūmal.*
    1969–1972. Oct. 23–Dec. 31 (microfilm).
    1973. Jan. 1–20 (microfilm).
    1975. Aug. 18–Sept. 27 (microfilm).
    1976. May 17 + (microfilm).

October star. d. est. Oct. 23, 1969.
  Note: Succeeds the *Somali news*. Ceased publication Feb. 12, 1970.
    1969-1970. Oct. 23-Feb. 12 (microfilm).

Ṣawt al-Ṣūmal.
  Note: In Arabic. Ceased publication Oct. 19, 1969. Succeeded by *Najmat Uktūbar*.
    1967-1969. Jan. 1-Oct. 19 (microfilm).

Somali news. w. est. Mar. 31, 1961.
  Note: Succeeds *Somaliland news*, Hargeisa. Ceased publication Oct. 22, 1969. Succeeded by *October star*.
    1961-1969. Mar. 31-Oct. 22 (microfilm).

Somalia courier; Corriere della Somalia. d.
  Note: In English, Italian and Arabic. Ceased publication sometime between Mar. 29-May 18, 1950. Succeeded by *Il Corriere della Somalia*.
    1945. Feb. 3-Dec. 31.
    1946. Jan. 2-July 1, Sept. 9-Dec. 6.
    1947. Nov. 17-Dec. 31.
    1948. Jan.-Nov. (fairly complete).
    1949-1950. Jan.-Mar. (fairly complete).

Stella d'Ottobre. d. est. Oct. 23, 1969.
  Note: Succeeds *Corriere della Somalia*. Ceased publication Jan. 20, 1973.
    1969-1973. Oct. 23-Jan. 20 (microfilm).

al-Ṭalīʻah. w.
  Note: In Arabic, English and Italian. Added title: *Horseed*.
    1970. Nov. 11 + (microfilm).

al-Waḥdah.
  Note: In Arabic.
    1966. Oct. 9 (sample issue).

Xiddigta Oktoobar. d. est. Jan. 21, 1973.
  Note: In Somali.
    1973. Jan. 21 + (microfilm).

South Africa

Bloemfontein

Friend. d. est. Mar. 16, 1896.
        1939. Nov. 25.
        1942. Sept. 28–Dec. 31.
        1943. Jan. 1–July 8 (incomplete).
        1944. Nov. 2–Dec. 30.
        1967. July–Dec. (microfilm).
        1968. Jan.–Feb., July–Dec. (microfilm).
        1970–1979. Sept.–Nov. (microfilm).

Goldfields friend. d. est. Sept. 1, 1956.
        1967–1971. Nov.–Feb. (incomplete microfilm).

Die Volksblad. w., s-w., d. est. Mar. 26, 1915.
  Note: In Afrikaans. Succeeds *Het Westen*, Potchefstroom.
        1953–1954. July 2–May 26 (fairly complete).
        1954. Oct. 27–Dec. 31.
        1955. Jan. 5, Mar. 21–Aug. 6 (incomplete).

Die Vrystater. s-w., w. est. May 31, 1941.
  Note: In Afrikaans.
        1949. July 30–Dec. 31.

Cape Town

Advance. w. est. May 1952.
  Note: Title until sometime between July 31 and Aug. 28, 1952, *Clarion*;
      until Nov. 6, 1952, *People's world*. Succeeded by *New age*, Oct. 28,
      1954.
        1952. Sept. 11–Oct. 30.
        1952–1954. Nov. 6–Oct. 21 (fairly complete microfilm).

Argus. d.
  Note: Continues the *Cape argus*.
        1969. Dec. 1 + (microfilm).

Die Burger. d. est. July 26, 1915.
  Note: In Afrikaans.
        1915–1945. July 26–Dec. (microfilm).
        1951. Mar. + (microfilm).

Cape argus. s-w., t-w., d. est. Jan. 3, 1857.
  Note: Continued by the *Argus*, Dec. 1, 1969.
           1863. Feb. 19, Apr. 20, May 9, Aug. 20.
           1939. Dec. 8.
           1944. Mar. 2–Dec. 27 (incomplete).
           1945–1946. Apr. 4–Mar. 30.
           1946–1948. Sept. 5–Sept. 30.
           1959–1961.
           1962–1969. Jan.–Nov. 29 (microfilm).

Cape argus; week-end edition.
           1899–1921. Dec. 27–Dec. 31.
           1922. Jan. 14–Apr. 29, July–Dec.
           1923–1942.
           1944. Mar. 4–Dec. 30.
           1945–1958. Apr. 7–Dec. 27.

Cape standard. w. est. May 11, 1936.
  Note: In English and Afrikaans. Ceased publication Nov. 25, 1947.
           1941–1943. Oct.–Dec. (incomplete).
           1944–1947. Jan.–Nov. 25.

Cape times. d. except Sunday. est. May 27, 1876.
           1912. Mar. 28.
           1938–1941. July–Aug. (microfilm).
           1942. Mar. 14–May.
           1942–1943. June–May (microfilm).
           1945. Feb. 10–Dec. 29 (incomplete).
           1946–1948 (fairly complete).
           1949 + (microfilm).

Cape times. w. est. Nov. 9, 1887.
           1899–1901. Nov. 8–Feb. 13 (fairly complete).

Cape Town mail, and mirror of court and council. w., s-w. est. Mar. 6, 1841.
  Note: Ceased publication June 28, 1853. Incorporated by the *South African commercial advertiser*, July 1853, which was then continued as the *South African commercial advertiser and Cape Town mail*.
           1842. Aug. 20.
           1843. Sept. 9, 23, 27, 30, Oct. 14, Nov. 11, 18.

Guardian. w. est. Feb. 19, 1937.
  Note: Title Feb. 19–June 11, 1937, *Cape guardian*. Succeeded by *Clarion* in May 1952.
           1941–1943. Oct. 9–June 3 (fairly complete).

Die Landstem. w. est. July 7, 1950.
  Note: In Afrikaans.
              1950. July 7-Oct. 28.
              1951. Apr. 28-May 19, Oct. 20, Nov. 10.
              1952. Mar. 15-Dec. 27 (fairly complete).
              1953. Jan. 3-Mar. 28, May 23-Dec. 26.
              1954. Jan. 2-Mar. 27.

New age. w. est. Oct. 28, 1954.
  Note: Succeeds *Advance*. Suspended publication Apr. 1-Sept. 1, 1960.
         Ceased publication Nov. 30, 1962. Succeeded by *Spark*.
              1954-1960. Oct. 28-Mar. 31.
              1960-1961. Sept.-Dec.
              1962. Jan.-Nov. (microfilm).

Progress. m. est. Feb. 1967.
  Note: In English and Afrikaans.
              1967-1979. Feb.-Dec. (microfilm).

South African advertiser and mail. 4w.
  Note: Succeeds the *South African commercial advertiser and Cape Town mail*.
         Ceased publication Sept. 29, 1869. Incorporated by the *Cape stan-
         dard and mail*.
              1863. Mar. 21, May 20, Nov. 18, 19, Dec. 5, 19.
              1864. Jan. 20, Feb. 20.

South African commerical advertiser. w., s-w. est. Jan. 7, 1824.
  Note: Suspended publication May 10, 1824-Aug. 31, 1825, and Mar.
         10, 1827-Oct. 3, 1828. Incorporated the *Cape Town mail, and mirror
         of court and council*, in July 1853, and was continued as the *South
         African commercial advertiser and Cape Town mail*.
              1840. June 17.
              1853. Apr. 23.

South African news. w.
              1900. Nov. 14.

Sun. w. est. Aug. 26, 1932.
  Note: In English and Afrikaans. Ceased publication Sept. 1956.
              1941-1942. Nov. 21-Dec. 11.
              1944. Jan. 28-Dec. 29.
              1945-1947. Jan. 5-Jan. 31 (incomplete).
              1950-1954. Dec. 1-Sept. 3.

Dundee

Northern Natal courier. w. est. 1904.
  Note: In English and Afrikaans.
          1948–1949.
          1950–1951 (fairly complete).

Durban

Daily news.
  Note: Continues the *Natal daily news*, Mar. 26, 1962.
          1967 + (microfilm).

Ilanga. w. est. Apr. 1903.
  Note: In English and Zulu.
          1945–1954.
          1964 (microfilm).
          1966. July–Dec. (microfilm).
          1972 (microfilm).
          Current issues held for one year only after 1972.

Leader. w. est. Sept. 1941.
          1974. Feb. 22 + (microfilm).

Natal daily news. est. 1878.
  Note: Incorporated the *Daily tribune*. Continued by the *Daily news*, Mar.
          26, 1962.
          1939. Nov. 30, Dec. 2.

Natal mercury. w., t-w., d. est. Nov. 25, 1852.
  Note: Title formerly *Natal mercury and commercial and shipping gazette*.
          1901–1904. Jan. 4–Dec. 30.
          1906–1909. Jan. 5–June 25.
          1939. Dec. 6.
          1941–1942. Nov. 13–Dec. 31 (fairly complete).
          1943. Jan. 28–June 16 (incomplete).
          1973 + (microfilm).

Post. w.
  Note: Continues the *Post*, Johannesburg. Continued by the *Post* (Natal
          ed.).
          1975–1978. July 27–July 12/16 (microfilm).

Post (Natal ed.). w.
  Note: Continues the *Post*.
          1978. July 19/23 + (microfilm).

Sunday tribune. est. Oct. 6, 1935.
   Note: Suspended publication Apr. 1939–June 1947.
                1972. Dec. 31 + (microfilm).

Weekend daily news. est. 1878.
   Note: Incorporated the *Sunday tribune.*
                1939. Dec. 2.

East London

Daily dispatch. est. Sept. 10, 1872.
                1955. Sept. 3.

Eshowe

Zululand star.
                1979. Apr. 12 (sample file).

Zululand times. w. est. 1907.
                1943–1944. May 13–Dec. 14 (incomplete).
                1945–1948.
                1949 (fairly complete).
                1950–1955.
                1956. Jan. 5–June 21, July 19, Aug. 16, Sept. 20, Oct. 11.
                1965. Sept. 9 (sample file).

Giyani (Kazankulu Homeland)

Mhalamhala. b-w? est. Sept. 20, 1978.
   Note: In English and the vernacular.
                1978. Sept. 20.
                1982. Mar. 3, 31, Apr. 14.

Greytown

Greytown gazette. w. est. 1904.
                1946–1952 (fairly complete).

Johannesburg

Afrikaner Idishe Tsaytung (African Jewish Newspaper). w. est. Apr. 10,
1931.
   Note: In Yiddish.
                1939. June 16, Sept. 8, Dec. 15.
                1979. May 25 +

Die Beeld. w., d. except Sunday. est. 1965.
  Note: In Afrikaans.
        1968. Feb. 25 (sample file).

Citizen d. est. Feb. 8, 1979.
  Note: Incorporated the *Financial gazette*.
        1979. Feb. 8 +

Dagbreek en Landstem. w. est. Oct. 4, 1970.
  Note: In Afrikaans. Formed by the merger of *Dagbreek en Sondagnuus* and
        Die Landstem. Ceased publication Nov. 22, 1970. Succeeded by
        Rapport.
        1970. Oct. 4–Nov. 22 (microfilm).

Dagbreek en Sondagnuus. w. est. June 29, 1947.
  Note: In Afrikaans. Title June 29–Dec. 7, 1947, *Dagbreek*. Incorporated
        Die Weekblad and *Sondagnuus*, Dec. 14, 1947. Ceased publication
        Sept. 27, 1970. Succeeded by *Dagbreek en Landstem*.
        1948–1950. Aug.–Dec. (fairly complete).
        1951. Jan.–Sept.
        1952. Jan. 6, 13, June 29.
        1952–1955. July 6–Mar. 27.
        1958. Oct. 26, Nov. 9–23.
        1959. Jan. 11, Feb. 1–Mar. 15, May 10, 24.
        1963–1970. Apr.–Sept. 27 (microfilm).

Financial gazette. w. est. May 27, 1977.
  Note: Continues the *South African financial gazette*. Ceased publication
        February 2, 1979. Incorporated by the *Citizen*.
        1977–1979. May 27–Feb. 2 (microfilm).

Forward. w. est. Dec. 11, 1924.
        1949. Jan. 7(m).

International. w. est. Sept. 10, 1915.
        1915–1924. Sept. 10–Sept. 5 (microfilm).

Jewish herald. w. est. Mar. 12, 1937.
  Note: Title until Nov. 26, 1937, *11th hour*.
        1952. Oct. 31.
        1963 + (microfilm).

Naledi ya batswana. w. est. Aug. 1944.
  Note: In Tswana and English. Suspended publication Dec. 1954–Aug.
    1958. Incorporated the *African echo* upon the resumption of publi-
    cation. Ceased publication Mar. 1964.
      1963–1964. June 15–Mar. 14 (microfilm).

Nation. m., irreg. est. Dec. 1976.
  Note: Ceased publication.
      1976–1979. Dec.–Dec. (microfilm).
      1980. Jan.–Feb., May.

Post. w. est. Mar. 27, 1955.
  Note: Title Mar. 27, 1955–Aug. 21, 1960, *Golden City post*. Continued by
    the *Post*, Durban.
      1963–1975. Jan.–July 20 (microfilm).

Post (Transvaal edition). d. est. Oct. 31, 1977.
  Note: Succeeds the *World*. Ceased publication Oct. 31, 1980.
      1978–1980. Aug.–Oct. (microfilm).

Rand daily mail. est. 1902.
      1963. Jan.–Sept., Dec. (microfilm).
      1964. Mar. + (microfilm).

Rapport. w. est. Nov. 29, 1970.
  Note: In Afrikaans. Succeeds *Dagbreek en Landstem*.
      1975 + (microfilm).

S. African Jewish times. w. est. July 17, 1936.
      1951. July 13, Aug. 3, 10, Oct. (Rosh Hashanah).
      1952. Feb. 8–Nov. 14.
      1953. Jan. 16–July 31 (incomplete).
      1964. June 5 (sample file).

Sandton chronicle.
      1973. Mid May issue (sample file).

South African financial gazette. w. est. Sept. 4, 1964.
  Note: Continued by the *Financial gazette*.
      1967–1977. Jan.–May 20 (microfilm).

Sowetan. d. est. Jan. 1981.
      1982. Feb. 23 (sample file).
      1982. Sept. +

Star. t-w., d. est. Oct. 17, 1887.
  Note: Title until Apr. 5, 1889, *Eastern star.*
              1945. Feb. 5-Apr. 21 (fairly complete).
              1951. Jan. 25-Mar. 3.
              1951-1953. Sept. 11-June 30 (fairly complete).
              1956. Sept. 18, 19, 22, 25, Oct. 2-15, Nov.-Dec.
              1957. Jan. 17-Apr. 30, July 3-Dec. 31.
              1958-1960.
              1961 (fairly complete).
              1962 + (microfilm).

Star (Weekly air edition).
              1965-1966. July 3-May 28 (microfilm).
              1967. Jan. 21-July 1 (microfilm).
              1968. June 22-Dec. 21 (microfilm).
              1969-1970. June 14-Jan. 10 (microfilm).

Sunday express. est. Mar. 4, 1934.
  Note: Title Mar. 4-July 29, 1934, the *Express.* Suspended publication
        Mar. 14, 1942-July 1945.
              1962. Dec. 2 + (microfilm).

Sunday post. est. Nov.? 1977.
  Note: Succeeds the *Weekend World.* Ceased publication Oct. 26, 1980.
              1978-1980. Aug.-Oct. (microfilm).

Sunday times. est. Feb. 4, 1906.
              1942. May 17-Dec. 27.
              1951. Feb. 25, Sept. 16-Nov. 11, Dec. 2, 23.
              1952-1954. Mar.-Dec. (fairly complete).
              1958-1959. Aug. 31-May 17 (incomplete).
              1962. Aug. 19, Dec. 2-30.
              1963-1966 (microfilm).
              1967-1968. Jan. 8-Jan. 7 (incomplete microfilm).
              1973 + (microfilm).

Die Transvaler. d. est. Oct. 1, 1937.
  Note: In Afrikaans.
              1937. Oct. 1(m).
              1952. Jan. 26-Apr. 30.
              1952-1955. Aug.-Aug. (fairly complete).
              1956 + (microfilm).

Umsebenzi; South African worker. w., m. est. July 2, 1926.
  Note: In English and the vernacular. Title until Apr. 18, 1930, *South African worker* and again assuming this title for June 1936–Mar. 19, 1938. Some issues were published in Cape Town. Ceased publication Mar. 19, 1938.
      1926–1938. July 2–Mar. 19 (microfilm).

Umteteli wa Bantu. w. est. May 1920.
  Note: In English, North Sotho, Xosa and Zulu. Suspended publication Nov. 11, 1944–Feb. 17, 1945. Ceased publication Dec. 31, 1955. Succeeded by the monthly, *Umteteli wa Bantue Goli*, beginning Mar./Apr. 1956.
      1941–1943. Oct. 4–June 19 (incomplete).
      1945–1950. Mar. 24–Dec. 29 (fairly complete).
      1951–1955.

Die Vaderland. s-w., t-w., d. est. 1916.
  Note: In Afrikaans. Title until Mar. 19, 1932, *Ons Vaderland*. Published in Pretoria until June 9, 1936.
      1944. Oct. 14, 30–Nov. 4, Dec. 28.
      1945–1946. Jan. 22–Dec. 29 (incomplete).
      1947. Jan.–May, Aug. 8, Sept. 27–Dec. (incomplete).
      1948–1949. Jan.–Aug. (fairly complete).
      1962–1970. Feb.–Dec. (microfilm).
      1971. Mar. (microfilm).

Voice. w.
      1981. July 8/14 (sample file).

Weekend world. est. June 30, 1968.
  Note: Ceased publication Oct. 16? 1977. Succeeded by the *Sunday post*.
      1968–1977. June 30–Feb. (incomplete microfilm).

World. w., b-w., d. est. Apr. 9, 1932.
  Note: In English and many vernacular languages. Title Apr. 1932–Dec. 1955, *Bantu world*. Suspended publication Nov. 4, 1944–Feb. 2, 1945. Ceased publication Oct. 19, 1977. Succeeded by *Post* (Transvaal edition).
      1941–1944. Oct. 4–June 3.
      1946. May 4(m).
      1957–1958. June 15–Dec. 27 (fairly complete).
      1962–1977. Jan.–Oct. 14 (incomplete microfilm).

Kimberley

Diamond fields advertiser. t-w., d. est. Mar. 23, 1878.
    1939. Dec. 16.

King William's Town

Imvo zabantsundu. w. est. Nov. 3, 1884.
    Note: In English and Xosa. Title Jan. 1895–Apr. 1898, *Imvo Neliso Lomsi*, Apr. 1898–Aug. 1901, *Imvo Zontsundu Neliso Lomsi*. Suspended publication Aug. 1901–Oct. 1902. Published in Johannesburg, Oct. 26, 1940–(1953), East London (1953)–(1956), and Johannesburg (1956)–(1957).
        1884–1903. Nov.–Dec. (microfilm).
        1905–1956. Jan.–Feb. 25 (microfilm).
        1956–1957. Mar.–Dec.
        1958–1963 (microfilm).
        1967 + (microfilm).

Ladybrand

Ladybrand courant and border herald. w. est. 1906.
    Note: Absorbed the *Lesotho news* (Maseru, Lesotho), sometime after June 2, 1970.
        1971. Nov. 26 (sample file).

Mafikeng (Republic of Bophuthatswana)

Mafikeng mail. w, d. s-w., irreg. est. Nov. 1, 1899.
        1899–1900. Nov.–May.
        1945–1967. Jan. 12–June 23 (microfilm).

Mariannhill

Umafrika. w. est. Oct. 1910.
    Note: In English and Zulu. Title Oct. 1910–(Dec.) 1928, *Izindaba Zabantu*.
        1949–1950. Jan. 8–Dec. 23 (incomplete).
        1951. Jan. 6–Dec. 8.
        1953–1958.
        1959. Jan. 3–24, June 27–Dec. 26.
        1960–1961.
        1962 + (microfilm).

Nelspruit

KaNgwane times. s-m. est. Apr. 18, 1980.
   Note: In English and Swazi.
            1982. May 14 (sample file).

Newcastle

Newcastle advertiser. s-w., w. est. 1901.
   Note: In English and Afrikaans.
            1946-1947 (fairly complete).
            1948-1953.
            1958-1959. Jan. 10-Feb. 13.

Newcastle morning herald and miners' advocate.
            1961. May 11.

Pietermaritzburg

Natal witness. w., s-w., t-w., d. est. Feb. 27, 1846.
            1909-1910.
            1940. Jan. 6.
            1951-1954. Jan. 31-Mar. 10 (Wed. issues only).
            1954-1955, Mar.-Dec. (Sat. issues only).
            1956-1957.
            1958-1961 (Sat. issues only).
            1962 + (microfilm).

Port Elizabeth

Eastern province herald. w., s-w., t-w., d. est. May 7, 1845.
            1944-1955. Sept.-Dec.
            1956. Jan. 2-Feb. 18, Apr. 16-Oct. 13.
            1964-1979. July-Apr. (microfilm).

Evening post. est. 1947.
            1955. Aug. 12.

Ons land. s-w., w. est. Oct. 27, 1939.
   Note: In Afrikaans.
            1946-1949.

Pretoria

Press. s-w., d. est. July 1889.
            1889-1899. July 16-Sept. 30 (microfilm).

Pretoria news. s-w., d. est. June 11, 1898.
        1955. Sept. 12.
        1967–1968. Aug.–Mar. (microfilm).
        1970 + (microfilm).

Die Volkstem. w., s-w., 4w., d. est. Aug. 8, 1873.
  Note: In English and Afrikaans. Ceased publication Mar. 30, 1951.
        1942. Oct. 15–Dec. 31 (incomplete).
        1943. Jan. 4–July 15 (fairly complete).

Rustenburg

Rustenburg herald. w. est. 1923.
  Note: In English and Afrikaans.
        1963. Feb. 8–May (microfilm).
        1963. July 5 (sample file).

Sibasa (Republic of Venda)

Thohoyandou. m. est. Apr. 1977.
  Note: In English, Venda, and Pedi.
        1981. May 4 (sample file).

Springs

Springs and Brakpan advertiser. w. est. 1917.
        1943. Feb. 26–Dec. 31.

Standerton

Christian recorder. w. est. July 6, 1951.
  Note: Subtitle: *The journal for unity, Southern Africa's recognized religious
      newspaper.*
        1960. Oct. 21.

Umtata (Republic of Transkei)

Territorial news. w. est. 1904.
  Note: Succeeds *Umtata herald.*
        1944–1945 (fairly complete).
        1946–1954.
        1955–1958. Jan. 6–Aug. 7 (incomplete).

Umthunywa. w. est. July 1937.
    Note: In English and Xosa. Ceased publication July 1966.
            1944 (incomplete).
            1945-1950 (fairly complete).
            1951-1953.

Vryheid

Vryheid gazette and district news. w.
    Note: In Afrikaans and English.
            1943. Dec. 31.
            1948-1953 (microfilm).
            1958-1965. Feb. 28-Dec. (microfilm).
            1967. Sept. 22 (sample file).

Walvis Bay (Namibia)

Namib times. s-w. est. 1958.
    Note: In English, Afrikaans and German.
            Current issues held for one year only.

Wynberg

Wynberg times and South African agriculturist.
            1902-1905. Jan. 4-Dec. 30.

Sudan

Juba

Nile mirror. w., s-w. est. Sept. 18, 1970.
    Note: Published in Khartoum until sometime between Oct. 27, 1974,
        and Jan. 10, 1975. Suspended publication June 1–Oct. 5, 1973.
        Ceased publication 1981?
            1970–1979. Sept. 18–Dec. 5 (microfilm).
            1980–1981. Dec. 20–Aug. 8 (microfilm).

Khartoum

al-Aḥrār.
    Note: In Arabic.
            1969. Dec. 16 (sample issue).

al-Akhbār.
    Note: In Arabic.
            1963. Aug. 19 (sample issue).

Akhbār al-usbū‘.
    Note: In Arabic.
            1969. Dec. 18 (sample issue).

al-‘Alam.
    Note: In Arabic.
            1965. July 23 (sample issue).

Anbā’ al-Sūdān.
    Note: In Arabic.
            1957. May 10 (sample issue).

al-Ayyām. d. est. 1953.
    Note: In Arabic.
            1970 + (microfilm).

al-I‘lān.
    Note: In Arabic.
            1972. Mar. 22 (sample issue).

Ishtirākī al-Kharṭūm.
    Note: In Arabic.
            1977. Aug. 20 (sample issue).

Kurdifān. w.
   Note: In Arabic.
      1975-1979. Apr. 18-Jan. 8 (microfilm).

al-Mīthāq al-Islāmī.
   Note: In Arabic.
      1967. June 16 (sample issue).

Morning news. est. 1954.
   Note: Suspended publication Sept. 16, 1963-Feb. 17, 1964. Ceased
      publication Apr. 4, 1969.
         1958-1959 (fairly complete).
         1960-1969. Jan.-Apr. 4 (microfilm).

al-Nās.
   Note: In Arabic.
      1963. Aug. 18 (sample issue).

al-Nidā.
   Note: In Arabic.
      1965. July 23 (sample issue).

Nile pilot.
      1966. Jan. 20 (sample file).

al-Qūwāt al-musallaḥah. w.
   Note: In Arabic.
      1974. Jan. 12 + (microfilm).

al-Ra'y al-'Āmm. d.
   Note: In Arabic. Ceased publication Aug. 23, 1974.
         1961 (microfilm).
         1968-1974. Jan. 5-Aug. 23 (microfilm).

al-Salām.
   Note: In Arabic.
      1976. Mar. 13 (sample issue).

al-Ṣarāḥah.
   Note: In Arabic.
      1961. Dec. 4 (sample issue).

Ṣawt al-Shabāb.
   Note: In Arabic.
      1977. May 25 (sample issue).

Ṣawt al-Sūdān. s-w.
    Note: In Arabic.
            1956 (microfilm).

Ṣawt al-ṭullāb.
    Note: In Arabic.
            1975. Nov. 1 (sample issue).

al-Ṣiḥāfah. d. est. 1961.
    Note: In Arabic.
            1970. Aug.-Dec. (microfilm).
            1973. June + (microfilm).

Sudan daily.
    Note: Ceased publication 196?
            1960. Dec. 4-20.
            1961. Jan. 11-July 5 (incomplete).
            1962. Apr. 29-Dec. 31 (incomplete).
            1963-1964. Jan.-June (fairly complete microfilm).

Sudan daily times.
            1956. Apr. 3-Oct. 7 (incomplete).

Sudan echo. d.
    Note: Ceased publication.
            1967-1968. Jan. 1-Aug. 2 (microfilm).

Sudan news. d.
            1969-1970. Apr.-Oct. (incomplete microfilm).

Sudan standard. d.
    Note: Suspended publication Sept. 10, 1971-Jan. 1, 1973. Ceased publi-
        cation July 9, 1973.
            1971-1973. Aug. 13-July 9 (incomplete microfilm).

Sudan standard. s-w., w. est. July 7, 1976.
    Note: Suspended publication Jan. 4, 1981?
            1976-1978. July 7-July 31 (microfilm).
            1978-1981. Aug. 7-Jan. 4 (incomplete).

Sudan star. d.
    Note: Ceased publication Jan. 30, 1954.
            1950-1954. Sept.-Jan. (fairly complete).

al-Thawrah.
Note: In Arabic.
        1963. Aug. 9 (sample issue).

al-Tilighrāf.
Note: In Arabic.
        1963. Aug. 14 (sample issue).

Uktūbar 21.
Note: In Arabic.
        1967. Jan. 29 (sample issue).

al-Ummah.
Note: In Arabic.
        1967. Oct. 20 (sample issue).

Wad Madani

al-Jazīrah.
Note: In Arabic.
        1971. Dec. 16 (sample issue).

Swaziland

Mbabane

The Swazi observer. w. est. 1981.
       1982. July 3 (sample file).

Times of Swaziland. w., d. est. June 5, 1897.
   Note: Published at Bremersdorp until Oct. 16, 1903. Suspended publication Oct. 14, 1899–Oct. 9, 1903 and Feb. 1909–Nov. 12, 1931.
       1943–1946. Jan. 7–Dec. 12 (incomplete).
       1948. July 8–22, Sept. 2, 9, Oct. 28, Nov. 18, 25.
       1949–1952. Mar. 17–Aug. 2 (incomplete).
       1955–1957. Dec.–Dec.
       1958 (fairly complete).
       1959–1960.
       1961 + (microfilm).

Tanzania

Arusha

Tanganyika post. b-w.
  Note: In English and Swahili.
          1963–1964. Mar. 27–Jan. 15 (incomplete microfilm).

Dar es Salaam

Baragumu.
  Note: In Swahili.
          1956. May 17, Dec. 2, 9, 23, 30.
          1957. Jan. 6–Mar. 10, 24, Apr. 21, July 14, Aug. 11, 25–Dec.
          15.

Daily news. est. Apr. 26, 1972.
  Note: Formed by the merger of the *Nationalist* and *Standard*.
          1972. Apr. 26 + (microfilm).

G.D.R. leo.
  Note: In Swahili.
          1970. [Saba Saba fair issue] (sample file).

Habari za leo. w.
  Note: In Swahili.
          1953–1956. Feb. 6–Feb. 24 (microfilm).

Mwafrika. w.
  Note: In Swahili.
          1959–1964. Nov.–Dec. (incomplete microfilm).

Mwangaza. d.
  Note: In Swahili.
          1956. Dec. 10–29.
          1957. Jan. 14–Dec. 14 (incomplete).
          1958 (fairly complete).

Mzalendo. w. est. Apr. 30, 1972.
  Note: In Swahili.
          1972. Apr. 30 + (microfilm).

Nationalist. d. est. Apr. 17, 1964.
   Note: Merged with the *Standard*, forming the *Daily news*.
      1964-1972. Apr. 17-Apr. 25 (microfilm).

Ngurumo. d.
   Note: In Swahili. Ceased publication Nov. 13, 1976.
      1967-1976. Jan.-Nov. 13 (microfilm).

Settler. w. est. Aug. 25, 1928.
      1928. Aug. 25.

Standard. d. est. 1929?
   Note: Incorporated the *Tanganyika times*, d., July 1, 1930. Title until
      Nov. 25, 1964, *Tanganyika standard*. Merged with the *Nationalist*,
      forming the *Daily news*.
      1941. Nov. 26, 29.
      1942-1944 (fairly complete).
      1945-1972. Jan.-Apr. 25 (microfilm).

Sunday news. w. est. Nov. 7, 1954.
      1956-1957. Jan. 8-Oct. 6 (fairly complete).
      1967 + (microfilm).

Tanganyika opinion. w. est. 1924.
   Note: In English and Gujarati.
      1944. Mar. 17-May 5, Oct.-Dec.
      1945. Jan.-Apr. (incomplete).
      1946-1947. Apr. 5-Dec. 19.
      1951-1953. Feb. 2-Feb. 6 (fairly complete).

Tanganyika standard. w. est. Jan. 1, 1930.
   Note: Incorporated the *Tanganyika times*, w., July 5, 1930.
      1930. July 5-19.
      1943. Aug. 20, 27.
      1944-1945. Feb. 5-May 5 (fairly complete).
      1950-1953. Apr. 8-Apr. 11 (incomplete).

Tanganyika times. d. est. Jan. 4, 1926.
   Note: Incorporated by the *Tanganyika standard*, d., July 1, 1930.
      1926. Jan. 4.

Tanganyika times. w. est. Nov. 19, 1919.
   Note: Title until Jan. 2, 1926, *Dar-es-Salaam times*. Incorporated by the
      Tanganyika standard, w., July 5, 1930.
      1924. Sept. 27.
      1925-1930. Oct. 10-June 27 (fairly complete).

Uhuru. w., d.
　　Note: In Swahili.
　　　　　　1969. Nov. 23, Dec. 7–21 (sample file).
　　　　　　1972. Apr. + (microfilm).

Urusi leo. w.
　　Note: In Swahili.
　　　　　　1969. Nov. 23, Dec. 7–21 (sample file).
　　　　　　1972. Apr. + (microfilm).

Zuhra. w. est. 1957?
　　Note: In Swahili.
　　　　　　1957–1960. Nov. 1–Mar. 4 (incomplete microfilm).

Miembeni

Jamhuri. irreg. est. July 1963.
　　Note: In the vernacular.
　　　　　　1963. July 20 (sample file).

Moshi

Kusare dunganya. w.
　　Note: In Swahili. Ceased publication Sept. 30, 1967.
　　　　　　1962–1964. Nov. 17–Feb. 8 (incomplete microfilm).
　　　　　　1967. Jan.–Sept. (microfilm).

Rukwa ruka. m.
　　Note: In Swahili.
　　　　　　1977. Jan. (sample file).

Tabora

Kiongozi. s–m. est. 1950.
　　Note: In Swahili. Later removed to Dar es Salaam.
　　　　　　1965. Mar. 1 (sample file).

Zanzibar

Adal insaf. s–w., w., d. est. 1948.
　　Note: In English, Gujarati, and Swahili. Ceased publication Jan. 1964.
　　　　　　1954. Sept. 18.
　　　　　　1955. Apr. 30, May 7, July 2, 23, 30.

Afrika kwetu. w. est. 1929.
　　Note: In English and Swahili.
　　　　　　1962–1965. Dec. 13–Sept. 2 (incomplete microfilm).

Kweli ikidhihiri uwongo hujitenga. w. est. Oct. 24, 1970.
Note: In Swahili. Succeeds *Kweupe* and *Ukombozi*.
Ceased publication Aug. 23, 1973.
1970-1973. Oct. 24-Aug. 23 (microfilm).

Kweupe. s-w., w.
Note: In Swahili. Ceased publication Oct. 2, 1970. Succeeded by *Kweli ikidihiri uwongo hujitenga*.
1964-1970. Jan.-Oct. 2 (microfilm).

Mwongozi. w. est. 1942.
Note: In English, Arabic and Swahili. Ceased publication Jan. 1964.
1963-1964. Jan. 4-Jan. 3 (incomplete microfilm).

Samachar. w. est. 1902.
Note: In English and Gujarati.
1944. Jan. 23.
1945-1946. Nov. 4-July 28.
1946. Sept. 22-Nov. 3.
1947-1960.
1961-1967. Jan.-Apr. 23 (microfilm).

Truth prevails where lies must vanish. w. est. Oct. 24, 1970.
Note: Ceased publication Aug. 23, 1973.
1970-1973. Oct. 24-Aug. 23 (microfilm).

Ukombozi. irreg. est. Feb. 9, 1970.
Note: In Swahili. Ceased publication Oct. 12, 1970. Succeeded by *Kweli ikidhihiri uwongo hujitenga*.
1970. Feb. 9-Oct. 12 (incomplete microfilm).

Zanzibar times. w.
Note: In English and Gujarati.
1956 (fairly complete).
1957. Jan. 6-June 23.

Zanzibar voice. w., d. est. 1922.
Note: In English and Gujarati.
1942-1944 (incomplete).
1945-1949. Mar. 8-Dec. 31.
1950-1951 (fairly complete).
1952-1956 (incomplete).
1957-1960.
1966. Nov. 6 (sample file).

Togo

Lomé

La Nouvelle marche. d. est. Nov. 30, 1979.
  Note: In French and Ewe. Succeeds *Togo presse*.
    1979. Nov. 30 + (microfilm).

Le Togo français. d. est. Oct. 7, 1943.
  Note: Ceased publication Oct. 5, 1956. Succeeded by *Le Togo républicain*.
    1951–1952. July–Sept. 5 (incomplete).
    1956. Jan. 1–Oct. 2 (incomplete).

Togo presse. w., d. est. Apr. 26, 1962.
  Note: In French and Ewe. Ceased publication Nov. 29, 1979. Succeeded
    by *La Nouvelle marche*.
    1962–1979. Apr. 26–Nov. 29 (microfilm).

Le Togo républicain. s-w. est. Oct. 9, 1956.
  Note: Succeeds *Le Togo français*.
    1956. Oct. 12, 19–27, Nov. 10–17(m).
    1958. July 16–Sept. 20, Oct. 1–Nov. 29, Dec. 17.

Tunisia

Tunis

L'Action. d. est. Nov. 1, 1932.
Note: Title Nov. 1, 1932, *L'Action tunisienne*.
1932. Nov. 1 [Reproduction] (sample file).
1963 + (microfilm).

al-Aḥad.
Note: In Arabic.
1965. May 5 (sample issue).

al-'Amal. d. est. 1934.
Note: In Arabic.
1961. Jan.–Aug. (microfilm).
1966 + (microfilm).

L'Avenir. w. est. Oct. 21, 1981.
1981. Oct. 21 (sample file).

Bilādī.
Note: In Arabic.
1976. May 16 (sample issue).

Il Corriere di Tunisi (Corriere Eurafrica). m.
Note: In Italian.
1981. Aug. (sample file).

Démocratie. m. est. 1978.
1979. Feb. 3 (sample file).

La Dépêche tunisienne. d. est. 1889.
Note: Ceased publication during 1961.
1941–1942. Dec. 15–Oct. 26 (fairly complete).
1944–1951. Jan. 16–Feb. 28.
1952. Jan. 9–Mar. 11, June 1, Aug. 2, 24, 31.
1952–1956. Sept. 1/2–Jan. 13.
1960–1961. June–Sept.

La Gazette d'Israël. w. est. 1938.
1948–1951. Jan.–June (incomplete).

Le Petit matin. d.
  Note:˙ Ceased publication Sept. 8, 1967.
        1951-1959.
        1960-1961. Jan. 27-Dec. 31 (fairly complete).
        1962-1965. Jan.-June (incomplete microfilm).
        1967. Jan. 1-Sept. 8 (microfilm).

La Presse de Tunisie. d. est. 1934.
        1950. Apr.-June, July 1-15, Sept.-Oct.
        1952. Jan. 9-Mar. 25, July 2, Aug. 24.
        1952-1954. Sept. 3-Dec. 31.
        1955-1956. Apr. 16-Aug. 30 (fairly complete).
        1960-1961. Oct.-Dec. (fairly complete).
        1966 + (microfilm).

al-Ra'y.
  Note: In Arabic.
        1977. Dec. 29 + (microfilm).

al-Ṣabāḥ.
  Note: In Arabic.
        1967. Jan. 18 (sample issue).

al-Ṣadá.
  Note: In Arabic.
        1976. Dec. 6 (sample issue).

al-Salām.
  Note: In Arabic.
        1965. May 9 (sample issue).

al-Shaʻb.
  Note: In Arabic.
        1966. Sept. 1 (sample issue).

Le Temps. d. est. 1975.
        1975. June 21 (sample file).
        1975. Nov. + (microfilm).

Tunis hebdo. est. 1974.
        1977-1978. May-Apr. (microfilm).
        1980. Mar. + (microfilm).

Tunis-midi. d. est. Dec. 13, 1948.
        1948. Dec. 13.

Tunis-soir. d.
  Note: In French and Arabic.
          1952. Jan. 9–Mar. 11, May 14–16, 18–20.
          1952–1953. Sept. 3–Dec. 31.

La Tunisie française. d.
  Note: Suspended publication (Jan. 1, 1942)–Jan. 16, 1944. Ceased
      publication Mar. 29, 1947. Succeeded by *Tunisie-France*.
          1944–1947. Jan. 16–Mar. 29.

Tunisie-France. d. est. June 2, 1947.
  Note: Succeeds *La Tunisie-française*.
          1947–1949. June–Dec.
          1950. Apr.–Sept., Dec.
          1951. Jan.–Feb.
          1952. Jan. 9–Mar. 24.
          1952–1953. Sept. 3–June 30.
          1953. July 1–Aug. 14(m), Dec. 7–23, 26–31.
          1954–1955. Jan.–June (fairly complete).

Uganda

Jinja

Kodheyo?
Note: In Ganda.
1965. Jan. 6 (sample file).

Kampala

African pilot. s-w.
Note: In English and Ganda.
1963. Aug. 10 (sample file).

Ag Afrika. w. est. 1st week Oct. 1980.
Note: In Ganda. Began a new numbering series with 3rd week Oct.
1980. Ceased publication.
1980-1981. Oct.-Mar. (microfilm).

Bukedde. w.
Note: In Ganda.
1981. June 24, July 3, 16 (sample file).

Dobozi lya Burganda; The Uganda voice. b-w., t-m. est. 1928.
Note: In English and Ganda.
1944. Feb. 15, Nov. 30.
1945. Apr. 30-June 30, July 31-Oct. 15.
1946. Jan. 15-Mar. 15.
1947-1948. Feb. 15-Sept. 30 (incomplete).

Financial times. w. est. Nov. 5, 1980.
Note: Began a new numbering series with the Apr. 21, 1981 issue.
1980. Nov. 5 (microfilm).
1981. Apr. 21, May 22, June 17, July 16 (microfilm).

Gampe. est. Oct. 6, 1981.
Note: In Ganda.
1981-1982. Oct. 6-Apr. 1 (microfilm).

Kalisoliiso. w. est. 1980.
Note: In Ganda. Ceased publication.
1980. Oct. 15-Dec. 8 (microfilm).

Kampala guardian. w. est. 1980.
  Note: Suspended publication Nov. 4, 1980–Aug. 18, 1981. Ceased
      publication Dec. 16, 1981?
         1980. Oct. 17, Nov. 4 (microfilm).
         1981. Aug. 18–Oct. 16 (microfilm).

Mbuga. t-w. est. 1982.
  Note: In Ganda.
         1982. Sept. 3 +

Mubaka. w. est. 1980.
  Note: In Ganda.
         1980–1981. Sept. 22–Feb. 5 (incomplete microfilm).

Munnansi. w. est. Apr. 4, 1981.
  Note: In Ganda.
         1981. Apr. 4–Sept. 9 (microfilm).

Munnansi. English ed. w. est. May 29, 1981.
         1981. May 29–Sept. 18 (microfilm).

Munno. d. est. 1911.
  Note: In Ganda. Suspended publication July 15–Oct. 19, 1972 and Aug.
      12, 1976–Jan. 1, 1977.
         1963. June + (microfilm).

Muzinge. irreg. est. 1980.
  Note: In Ganda. Ceased publication.
         1980. 2nd Sept. week–Dec. 5 (microfilm).

Mwebembezi. w. est. 1963.
  Note: In Nyoro and Tooro. Ceased publication.
         1967–1977. Jan.–Aug. 19 (microfilm).
         1977. Sept. 9, 23, 30 (sample file).
         1978. June 16, Oct. 6 (sample file).

Ngabo. w. est. Feb. 1? 1980.
  Note: In Ganda.
         1980. Feb. 15 + (microfilm).

Omukulembeze. d. est. 1963.
  Note: In Ganda. Ceased publication.
         1967–1975 (microfilm).
         1976. Mar. 11 (sample file).

People. w., d.
  Note: Ceased publication June 2, 1973.
          1967-1973. Jan.-June 2 (microfilm).

People. w. est. Oct. 3, 1980.
  Note: Suspended publication Oct. 2, 1981.
          1980-1981. Oct. 3-Oct. 2 (incomplete microfilm).

Saba saba. w.
  Note: In Ganda.
          1980-1981. Apr. 14-July 24 (incomplete microfilm).

Star.w. est. Sept. 3, 1980.
          1980-1981. Sept. 3-Mar. 17 (incomplete microfilm).

Sunday times. est. Nov. 22, 1981.
          1981-1982. Nov. 22-Mar. 14 (incomplete microfilm).

Sunday voice. est. Dec. 17, 1978.
  Note: Ceased publication Mar. 18, 1979.
          1978-1979. Dec. 17-Mar. 18 (incomplete microfilm).

Taifa empya. 5w. est. 1961.
  Note: In Ganda.
          1963-1964 (microfilm).
          1967-1975. Jan.-Apr. (microfilm).
          1977 + (microfilm).

Taifa Uganda empya. w.
  Note: In Ganda.
          1963-1964 (microfilm).
          1967-1975. Jan.-Apr. (microfilm).
          1977 + (microfilm).

Uganda argus. d. est. 1955.
  Note: Succeeds the *Uganda herald*. Ceased publication Dec. 1, 1972. Suc-
          ceeded by the *Voice of Uganda*.
          1955-1956. Jan. 6-Feb. 28 (incomplete).
          1956-1972. Mar. 7-Dec. 1 (microfilm).

Uganda eyogera. w. est. Aug. 1980.
  Note: In Ganda. Ceased publication.
          1980. Aug.-Nov. 13 (incomplete microfilm).

Uganda nation. d. est. 1962.
  Note: Ceased publication Oct. 27, 1963.
          1963. Jan. 1-Oct. 27 (microfilm).

Uganda news. est. Sept. 4, 1925.
      1925. Sept. 4.

Uganda pilot. w. est. Oct. 30, 1980.
  Note: Suspended publication Nov. 21, 1980–Apr. 13, 1981 and June
     19–Dec. 4, 1981. Established a new numbering series after each of
     these suspensions.
     1980. Oct. 30 + (microfilm).

Uganda post. w. est. Aug. 6, 1981.
  Note: In Ganda.
     1981. Aug. 6 + (microfilm).

Uganda post. 4w. est. Feb. 1, 1982.
  Note: In Ganda.
     1982. Feb. 1 + (microfilm).

Uganda times. d. est. 1979.
  Note: Succeeds the *Voice of Uganda.*
     1979. May + (microfilm).

Uganda weekly news. est. Dec. 11, 1977.
  Note: Ceased publication Dec. 10, 1978.
     1977–1978. Dec. 11–Dec. 10 (microfilm).

Voice of Uganda. d. est. Dec. 2, 1972.
  Note: Succeeds the *Uganda argus.* Ceased publication Mar. 28, 1979.
     Succeeded by the *Uganda times.*
     1972–1979. Dec. 2–Mar. 28 (microfilm).

Weekly topic. est. May 11, 1979.
  Note: Ceased publication Mar. 31, 1981.
     1979–1981. May 11–Mar. 31 (microfilm).

The Weekly walker. est. July 13, 1981.
     1981. July 13, Aug. 5 (sample file).

Masaka

Agafa e buddu. w. est. 1980.
  Note: In Ganda.
     1980–1981. Sept. 18–May (microfilm).

Upper Volta

Ouagadougou

Carrefour africain. w. s-m. est. 1960.
        1961. May 7 + (microfilm).

L'Observateur. d. est. 1973.
        1977 + (microfilm).

Zaire

Bukavu

Centre-Afrique. w., d.
  Note: Ceased publication 196?
      1944–1948. Sept. 14–Dec. 30.

L'Echo du Kivu. w.
      1945–1952.

JUA. w. est. 1972.
  Note: In French.
      1973. Feb. 10/16 + (microfilm).

Kananga

Nsambi. w. est. 1976.
  Note: In French and Luba.
      1976. July 17 (sample file).

Kinshasa

L'Avenir. d.
  Note: Title (Apr. 27/28, 1941)–Feb. 10, 1955, *L'Avenir colonial belge*.
      1942. May 29–30.
      1944–1956. Jan. 1–Mar. 20 (incomplete).

Congo. w., d.
  Note: In French.
      1960. Apr. 23, Aug. 31, Sept. 1.

Le Courrier d'Afrique. d. est. Jan. 12, 1930.
  Note: Ceased publication Jan. 24/25, 1970. Succeeded in 1971? by a
      publication with the same title.
      1941–1943. Sept. 9–Feb. 19 (microfilm).
      1943–1955. Feb. 14/15–Dec. 30/31 (incomplete).
      1956–1970. Jan.–Jan. 23 (microfilm).
      1970. Jan. 24/25.

Le Courrier d'Afrique. d. est. 1971?
  Note: Succeeds an earlier publication with the same title. Ceased publi-
      cation Mar. 1972. Succeeded by *Elima*.
      1972. Jan. 5–Mar. 4/5 (microfilm).

125

Elima. d. est. Mar. 1972.
Note: In French. Succeeds *Le Courrier d'Afrique*.
1972. June + (microfilm).

Elombe. d. est. 1972.
Note: In French. Succeeds *La Tribune Africaine*.
1972. June 30–July 19 (incomplete microfilm).

L'Etoile du Zaire. d. est. Aug. ? 1963.
Note: Title until July 1, 1968, *L'Etoile du Congo*. Ceased publication
Mar. 5, 1972. Succeeded by *Myoto*.
1965–1972. Jan.–Mar. 5 (microfilm).

Mambenga.
Note: In French.
1973. Nov. 3 (sample file).

Myoto. d. est. Mar. 6, 1972.
Note: In French. Succeeds *L'Etoile du Zaire*.
1972. Mar. 6–July 18 (microfilm).

Nsango ya bisu. s-m.
Note: In French and Lingala.
1950. Oct. 1, Dec. 1.
1951 (incomplete).
1952. Apr. 1–May 1.

Présence congolaise. w. est. Dec. 22, 1956.
1956–1967. Dec. 22–Dec. 30 (incomplete microfilm).

Le Progrès. d. est. 1962?
Note: Ceased publication Mar. 5, 1972. Succeeded by *Salongo*.
1962–1972. Oct. 23–Mar. 5 (microfilm).

Salongo. d. est. Mar. 6, 1972.
Note: In French. Succeeds *Le Progrès*.
1972. Mar. 6 + (microfilm).

La Tribune Africaine. d.
Note: Title until sometime between Nov. 23, 1967 and Jan. 11, 1968, *La
Tribune*. Ceased publication Mar. 6, 1972. Succeeded by *Elombe*.
1967–1972. July 5–Mar. 6 (incomplete microfilm).

Umoja. w. est. 1972.
  Note: In French and Swahili.
        1973-1975. Jan. 6-May 10 (microfilm).

De Week.
  Note: In Flemish.
        1955. July 3.

Kisangani

L'Echo de Stan. d., s-w.
        1944-1953. Jan. 3-Aug. 13/16 (fairly complete).

La Gazette.
        1965. Mar. 9, 11 (sample file).

Le Stanleyvillois. s-w., d.
        1950-1960. Dec. 20-July 14 (fairly complete).

Lubumbashi

La Dépêche. d.
  Note: Suspended publication Dec. 12, 1965-Mar. 9, 1966, May 31-
        June 30 and Dec. 3-16, 1970. Ceased publication in 1972. Suc-
        ceeded by *Mwanga*.
        1965-1972. Mar.-Jan. (incomplete microfilm).

L'Echo du Katanga. d. est. 1930.
        1944-1956.
        1957-1958 (fairly complete).
        1959. Jan. 2-17, 21-Feb. 10, 12-26.
        1960-1961. June 14-June 10 (incomplete).
        1962-1964. Dec. 17-Aug. 10 (incomplete microfilm).

L'Essor du Congo. d. est. Mar. 8, 1928.
  Note: Ceased publication Dec. 1960. Succeeded by *L'Essor du Katanga*.
        Resumed this title with Mar. 7, 1967. Continued as *L'Essor du
        Zaire*, Oct. 30, 1971.
        1942-1943. Nov. 23-Apr. 2 (microfilm).
        1944-1960 (microfilm).
        1967-1971. Mar. 7-Oct. 29 (microfilm).

L'Essor du Katanga. d. est. Jan. 1961.
  Note: Succeeds *L'Essor du Congo*, again becoming that title with the Mar.
        7, 1967 issue.
        1961-1967. Jan.-Mar. 6 (microfilm).

L'Essor du Zaire. d.
> Note: Continues *L'Essor du Congo*. Ceased publication in 1972. Succeeded by *Taifa*.
> 1971–1972. Oct. 30–Jan. (microfilm).

Mjumbe. d. est. June 16, 1976.
> Note: In French and Swahili. Succeeds *Mwanga*.
> 1976. June 16 + (microfilm).

Mwanga. w., d. est. 1972.
> Note: In French. Succeeds *La Dépêche*. Ceased publication June 1976. Succeeded by *Mjumbe*.
> 1972–1975. Dec.–Dec. (microfilm).
> 1976. Jan.–June 12/13.

Taifa. d. est. 1972.
> Note: In French. Succeeds *L'Essor du Zaire*.
> 1973–1975. Jan.–July 13 (incomplete microfilm).

La Voix du Katanga. d. est. 1961?
> Note: Ceased publication during 1972. Succeeded by *Ukweli*.
> 1965–1971. Mar.–Dec. 18 (incomplete microfilm).

Zambia

Livingstone

Intanda. s-m. est. Jan. 1966.
Note: In English and Tonga (Zambesi).
1966 + (microfilm).

Livingstone mail. w. est. Mar. 31, 1906.
Note: Ceased publication May 30, 1968.
1944–1945. Jan. 7–Apr. 20.
1946–1948. Apr. 5–Dec. 31 (fairly complete).
1949 (incomplete).
1950. Jan.–Sept.
1951. May 25, Aug. 17, Oct. 5, Nov. 16.
1952 (fairly complete).
1953–1954.
1955. Feb. 22–Mar. 25, Apr. 26–Nov. 11, 22, 25.
1956–1957.
1958 (fairly complete).
1959. Jan.–May.
1967–1968. Jan.–May 30 (microfilm).

South-Western star. est. June 28, 1961.
1965. Dec. 22 (sample file).

Zambezi news. m.
1956. Feb. 8, Mar. 7, Apr. 11, June 6, July 4.

Lusaka

Central African mail. w. est. 1960.
Note: Title until Feb. 27, 1962, *African mail*. Succeeded by the *Zambia mail* on Aug. 13, 1965.
1961–1965. July–July (microfilm).

Central African post. t-w? est. Apr. 12, 1948.
Note: Ceased publication Feb. 28, 1964.
1955–1957. Oct. 5–Sept. 16.
1959–1964. Mar. 18–Feb. 28 (microfilm).

Mutende. est. Mar. 1936.
1952. Dec. 2.

Northern star. w. est. Mar. 1, 1963.
    Note: Ceased publication Oct. 15, 1964. Succeeded by the *Zambia star.*
        1963-1964. Mar. 1-Oct. 15 (microfilm).

Weekend world. est. 1978.
        1978. July 14 (sample file).

Zambia daily mail.
    Note: Continues the *Zambia mail,* Sept. 1, 1970.
        1970. Sept. 1 + (microfilm).

Zambia evening mail. d. est. Oct. 23, 1974.
    Note: Ceased publication Oct. 25, 1974.
        1974. Oct. 23-25 (microfilm).

Zambia mail. w., s-w., d. est. Aug. 13, 1965.
    Note: Succeeds the *Central African mail.* Continued by the *Zambia daily mail,* Sept. 1, 1970.
        1965-1970. Aug. 20-Aug. (microfilm).

Zambia star. w. est. Oct. 22, 1964.
    Note: Succeeds the *Northern star.*
        1964. Oct. 22-Dec. 24 (microfilm).

Mongu

Liseli. b-w., m., irreg.
    Note: In Lozi. Title until sometime in 1978, 1979, or 1980, *Liseli la Zambia.*
        1972-1975 (incomplete microfilm).
        1976-1978 (incomplete).
        1980 + (incomplete).

Ndola

Northern news. d. except Sunday. est. 1943.
    Note: Ceased publication June 30, 1965. Succeeded by the *Times of Zambia.*
        1957. Jan.-July (incomplete).
        1957-1958. Oct. 14-Dec. 31 (fairly complete).
        1959. Jan.-Aug. (incomplete).
        1959-1961. Sept.-Sept.
        1963-1965. Jan.-Apr. (microfilm).

Sunday times of Zambia. est. Nov. 1, 1970.
  Note: Succeeds the *Zambia news*.
        1970. Nov. 1 + (microfilm).

Times of Zambia. d. except Sunday. est. July 1, 1965.
  Note: Succeeds the *Northern news*.
        1967 + (microfilm).

Zambia news. w. est. Oct. 6, 1963.
  Note: Place of publication varies. Ceased publication Dec. 29, 1968?
        1964-1965. Jan. 5-Feb. 28 (incomplete microfilm).
        1965-1968. Mar. 7-Dec. 29 (incomplete).

Zimbabwe

Bulawayo

Chronicle. w., s-w., d. est. Oct. 12, 1894.
  Note: Title until June 15, 1951, *Bulawayo chronicle.*
    1939. Nov. 29, Dec. 1.
    1946. Sept. 13.
    1947-1949. June 6-Sept. 30.
    1949. Oct.-Dec.
    1950. Jan. 3-Feb. 23 (incomplete).
    1953. July 3.
    1957. Feb. 6, June 22, Aug. 17-26.
    1959. Nov. 4-Dec. 31.
    1960 + (microfilm).

Gweru

Moto. w., m. est. Oct. 1959.
  Note: In English, Shona and Ndebele.
    1970-1974 (incomplete microfilm).
    1980. Jan. 26-Aug. 9 (incomplete).
    1982. June +

Harare

African weekly. est. June 7, 1944.
  Note: Ceased publication Jan. 1962. Succeeded by *Daily news*; weekend
    edition, Feb. 2, 1962.
    1944. June-Dec. (incomplete).
    1945-1957.
    1958. Apr. 16, Sept. 24-Dec. 31.
    1959-1962. Jan.-Jan.

Bantu mirror. qtly., m., w. est. Jan. 1931.
  Note: In English, Ndebele, and Shona. Title until Feb. 15, 1936, *Native
    mirror.* Removed from Bulawayo, Nov. 25, 1944. Ceased publica-
    tion Jan. 1962. Succeeded by *Daily news*; weekend edition.
    1940-1944. Jan. 6-Dec. 30.
    1956-1957. Mar. 10-Feb. 16.
    1959-1962. July 4-Jan. 27.

Bwalo la Nyasaland. w.
   Note: In English and Nyanja. Ceased publication. Succeeded by *Bwalo*.
      1955. Oct. 11.

Daily news.
   Note: Title formerly *Central African daily news, African daily news*. Banned
      by the government as of Aug. 28, 1964.
         1958–1961. Feb.–Dec. (fairly complete).
         1962–1964. Jan.–Aug. 27 (microfilm).

Daily news; weekend edition. est. Feb. 1962.
   Note: Published in two editions; for Southern Rhodesia in English and
      Shona, for Northern Rhodesia and Nyasaland in English and
      Nyanja. Title formerly *Central African daily news, The African daily
      news*. Succeeded the *African weekly, African weekly recorder, Bantu mirror*, and the *Harvester*.
         1962–1964. Feb. 2–Aug. 22 (microfilm).

The Drums of Zimbabwe. t-w., s-w. est. 1978.
   Note: In English and the vernacular.
         1978–1979. Oct. 13–Oct. 24 (incomplete microfilm).

Financial gazette. w. est. Apr. 1970.
         1977. May + (microfilm).

Herald. d. est. Aug. 15, 1978.
   Note: Continues the *Rhodesia herald*. d.
         1978. Aug. 15 + (microfilm).

National observer. w.
   Note: Ceased publication Aug. 8, 1980.
         1978–1980. Jan.–Aug. 8 (microfilm).

New star. w. est. Dec. 3, 1976.
   Note: Ceased publication during 1978.
         1976–1977. Dec. 10–May 27 (incomplete microfilm).

Rhodesia herald. d. est. Oct. 1892.
   Note: Incorporated the *Evening standard*. Continued by the *Herald*.
         1927–1950. Jan.–May (microfilm).
         1953–1955.
         1956–1978. Jan.–Aug. 14 (microfilm).

Rhodesia herald. w.
         1943–1955. Jan.–June.

Sunday mail. est. June 2, 1935.
       1967. Oct. 22 (sample file).
       1973 + (microfilm).

Zimbabwe times. w.
   Note: Banned by the government as of Oct. 2, 1978.
       1977–1978. Apr.–Oct. 2 (microfilm).

Title Index

A

ABC Diário de Angola, 5
A.E.F., 15
Abidjan-matin, 41
Action (Port-Louis), 62
L'Action (Tunis), 117
Action Réunionnaise, 86
Actualité, 19
Actuel, 54
Adal insaf, 114
al-'Adālah, 65
Addis-soir, 30
'Adis Zaman, 30
Advance (Cape Town), 94
Advance (Port-Louis), 62
Advance (Yaba), 84
Ady-gasy, 54
Āfāq siyāsīyah, 68
Africa samachar, 43
Africa times, 43
African daily news, 133
African Jewish newspaper, 98
African morning post, 35
African national times, 35
African nationalist, 47
African pilot, 120
African spectator, 35
African standard, 43
African weekly, 132
Africa's luminary, 47
Afrika kwetu, 114
Afrikaner Idishe Tsaytung, 98
Ag Afrika, 120
Agafa e buddu, 123
al-Ahad, 117
al-Ahdāf, 65
al-Ahrām, 19
al-Ahrār (Cairo), 19
al-Ahrār (Khartoum), 107
al-Ahrār (Tanta), 28
Aimiro, 30
al-Akhbār (Cairo), 19
al-Akhbār (Khartoum), 107
al-Akhbār (Rabat), 69
Akhbār al-'ummāl, 19
Akhbār al-usbū', 107
Akhbār al-yawm, 19
Ako takariva, 54
al-'Alam (Addis Ababa), 30
al-'Alam (Cairo), 20
al-'Alam (Khartoum), 107
al-'Alam (Rabat), 69
Albishir (Maiduguri), 83
Albishir (Zaria), 84
Alger ce soir, 1
Alger républicain, 1
Alger-soir, 1
Allgemeine Zeitung, 76
al-'Amal (Benghazi), 50
al-'Amal (Tunis), 117
Amana, 80
Anatole, 18
al-Anbā', 69
Anbā' al-Jīah, 20
Anbā' al-Sūdān, 107
Angola norte, 5
O Apostolado, 5
O Arauto, 40
al-Ard, 51
Arev, 20
Argus, 94
Asdā', 69
Ashanti pioneer, 37
Ashanti sentinel, 38
Ashanti times, 38
Atlantic courier, 65
Atrika, 54
L'Aube, 62
L'Aube nouvelle du Dahomey, 7
L'Aurore, 58
L'Avenir (Kinshasa), 125
L'Avenir (Tunis), 117
al-Ayyām (Khartoum), 107
al-Ayyām (Tripoli), 51

B

al-Ba'kūkah al-jadīdah, 20
al-Balāgh, 20
Bantu mirror, 132
Bantu world, 102
Baragumu, 112
Baraza, 43
Barisā, 30
al-Barlamān, 69
Barqah al Jadīdah, 50
al-Basā'ir, 1
Basutoland news, 46
Bas'y-vava, 54
al-Bayān, 65
al Bayane, 65
Die Beeld, 99

135

Beira news, 74
al-Bilād, 51
Bilādī, 117
Bong crier, 47
Bornu people, 84
La Bourse égyptienne, 20
O Brado africano, 74
Bukedde, 120
Bulawayo chronicle, 132
Būr Sa'īd, 27
Die Burger, 94
Business times, 81
Bwalo la Nyasaland, 133

C

Cameroon chronicle, 10
Cameroon panorama international, 10
Cameroon times, 10
Cameroon tribune (d), 10
Cameroon tribune (w), 11
Le Cameroun libre, 11
Canard Déchaine, 14
Cape argus, 95
Cape argus (week-end ed.), 95
Cape guardian, 95
Cape standard, 95
Cape times (d), 95
Cape times (w), 95
Cape Town mail, and mirror of court
    and council, 95
Carrefour africain, 124
Central Africa review, 45
Central African daily news, 133
Central African mail, 129
Central African post, 129
Central African times, 59
Centre-Afrique, 125
Le Cernéen, 62
al-Chaab (Algiers), 1
Chaab (Nouakchott), 61
Chemsa bongo, 43
Christian recorder, 105
Chronicle, 132
La Chronique congolaise, 9
Citizen, 99
Clarion, 94
Coastweek, 42
Colonial times, 43
Combate, 74
O Comercio, 6
Congo, 125
Correspondance d'Ethiopie, 30
Corriere dell'Impero, 30
Il Corriere della Somalia, 92

Corriere di Tripoli, 51
Il Corriere di Tunisi (Corriere
    Eurafrica), 117
La Côte d'Ivoire, 41
Le Courrier d'Afrique, 125
Le Courrier d'Ethiopie, 30
Courrier de l'Algérie, 1
Le Courrier de Madagascar, 54
Le Courrier du Maroc, 68
Croix sud, 86
Cronaca, 18
Cyrenaica observer, 50
Cyrenaica weekly news, 50

D

Dagbreek en Landstem, 99
Dagbreek en Sondagnuus, 99
Daho express, 7
Daily chronicle, 43
Daily comet (Kano), 81
Daily comet (Lagos), 81
Daily dispatch, 98
Daily echo, 35
Daily express, 81
Daily graphic, 35
Daily mail (Freetown), 91
Daily mail (Kano), 81
Daily nation, 43
Daily news (Dar es Salaam), 112
Daily news (Durban), 97
Daily news (Gaborone), 8
Daily news (Harare), 133
Daily news; weekend ed., 133
Daily observer, 47
Daily service, 82
Daily sketch, 79
Daily star, 78
Daily telegraph, 82
Daily times (Blantyre), 59
Daily times (Lagos), 82
Daily times (Monrovia), 47
Dakar-Matin, 89
Dar-es-Salaam times, 113
Dawn, 92
La Démocratie (Saint-Denis), 86
Démocratie (Tunis), 117
La Démocratie populaire, 54
La Dépêche, 127
La Dépêche algérienne, 1
La Dépêche d'Algérie, 1
La Dépêche de Constantine et de
    l'est algérien, 3
La Dépêche de l'est, 3
Dépêche du Ruanda-Urundi, 9
La Dépêche marocaine, 72

La Dépêche quotidienne d'algérie, 2
La Dépêche tunisienne, 117
Dernière heure, 2
Les Dernières nouvelles, 2
Deutsche Orient-zeitung, 20
El Día, 73
Diamond fields advertiser, 103
Diário, 74
Diario de Africa, 73
Diário de Luanda, 6
Diário de Moçambique, 74
Dimanche matin, 2
Dipanda, 15
Dobozi lya Burganda; The Uganda
    voice, 120
Drums of Zimbabwe, 133

E

East African standard (d), 43
East African standard (w), 44
Eastern Nigeria guardian, 84
Eastern observer, 83
Eastern outlook, 79
Eastern outlook and Cameroons star, 79
Eastern province herald, 104
Eastern sentinel, 78
Eastern star, 101
Eastern states express, 78
Ebano, 29
L'Echo d'Alger, 2
L'Echo d'Oran, 4
L'Echo de Stan., 127
L'Echo de Tanger et de la
    Méditerranée, 72
L'Echo des Îles, 90
Echo-dimanche, 4
L'Echo du dimanche, 4
L'Echo du Katanga, 127
L'Echo du Kivu, 125
L'Echo du Maroc, 69
Echo-soir, 4
Echos, 20
Ecos de Angola, 6
Egyptian gazette, 20
Egyptian mail, 21
Egyptian standard, 21
Ehuzu, 7
11th hour, 99
Elima, 126
Elombe, 126
L'Equateur, 15
Eritrean daily news, 31
España, 72
L'Essor, 60

L'Essor du Congo, 127
L'Essor du Katanga, 127
L'Essor du Zaire, 128
L'Etendard égyptien, 21
Ethiopian herald, 30
L'Etoile du Congo, 126
L'Etoile du Zaire, 126
Etumba, 15
L'Eveil du Cameroun, 10
Evening news (Accra), 35
Evening news (Nairobi), 44
Evening post, 104
Express (Johannesburg), 101
Express (Monrovia), 47
L'Express (Port-Louis), 62

F

al-Fadā'ih, 69
al-Fajr, 92
Al-Fajr al-Jadīd, 51
al-Fallāh, 69
Fanal, 86
Fandrosoana, 54
El Faro, 68
Fās, 68
al-Fātih, 51
Fazzān, 51
al-Fidā' al-jadīd, 21
Filastin, 65
Financial gazette (Harare), 133
Financial gazette (Johannesburg), 99
Financial punch, 80
Financial times, 120
Forward, 99
France-Afrique (Abidjan), 41
France-Afrique (Brazzaville), 15
France-Dahomey, 7
France-équateur l'avenir, 15
France-Madagascar, 55
Fraternité hebdo, 41
Fraternité matin, 41
Friend (Bloemfontein), 94
Friend (Monrovia), 47

G

G.D.R. leo, 112
Gabon d'aujourd'hui, 33
Gambia echo, 34
Gambia news bulletin, 34
Gambia outlook (In miniature), 34
Gambia outlook and Senegambian
    reporter, 34

Gambia times, 34
Gampe, 120
Gasikara vaovao, 55
Gaskiya ta fi Kwabo (Kaduna), 81
Gaskiya ta fi Kwabo (Zaria), 84
Gazetin 'ny Malagasy, 55
La Gazette, 127
La Gazette d'Israël, 117
La Gazette d'orient, 18
Gazety roso, 55
Gazety sariaka, 55
Gboungboun, 79
Ghana daily express, 35
Ghana daily mail, 36
Ghana evening news, 36
Ghana star, 36
Ghana times, 36
Ghanaian times, 36
Giornale dell'Eritrea, 31
Il Giornale di Tripoli, 51
Goan voice, 44
Gold Coast commercial guardian, 36
Gold Coast daily graphic, 36
Gold Coast independent, 36
Gold Coast news, 37
Gold Coast observer and weekly
    advertiser, 37
Goldfields friend, 94
Greytown gazette, 98
Guardian (Cape Town), 95
Guardian (Victoria), 10
Guidance, 36
Guinea times, 36
La Guinée française, 39

                        H

Habari za leo, 112
Hādhihi al-dunyā, 68
al-Ḥaqā'iq, 21
al-Ḥaqīqah, 50
al-Ḥarakah, 69
Hazolava, 55
L'Hebdo, 86
Hebrat, 31
Heegan, 92
Hehy, 55
Herald (Harare), 133
Herald (Monrovia), 47
Hindu, 64
al-Ḥiwār, 18
Hoja del Lunes de Fernando Poo, 29
L'Homme nouveau; kongo ya sika, 15
Horizons nouveaux, 62
Horoya, 39

Horseed, 93
Housaper, 21
Hsin shang pao (New Chinese
    commerical paper), 63
al-Ḥurrīyah (Cairo), 21
al-Ḥurrīyah (Rabat), 69
al-Ḥurrīyah (Tripoli), 52

                        I

al-I'lām, 21
al-I'lān, 107
Ilanga, 97
Imongo Vaovao, 55
Imvo neliso lomza, 103
Imvo zabantsundu, 103
Imvo zontsundu, 103
Independent, 47
India news, 36
L'Informateur, 18
Intanda, 129
International, 99
O Intransigente, 5
Irohin Yoruba, 79
Isan' andro, 55
Ishtirākī al-Kharṭūm, 107
al-Ithnayn, 70
al-I'tidāl, 21
al-Ittiḥād al-waṭanī, 65
'Ityopyā, 32

                        J

JUA, 125
Jakadiya, 85
Jamhuri, 114
al-Janūb, 70
al-Jarīdah al-'Arabīyah al-usbū'īyah, 32
al-Jarīdah al-tijārīyah al-Misrīyah, 21
Jarīdat Misr, 22
al-Jazīrah, 110
Jewish herald, 99
al-Jihād (Cairo), 22
al-Jihād (Tripoli), 52
Joernaal, 76
Jornal de Angola, 6
Jornal de Benguela, 5
Jornal do Congo, 6
Le Journal, 2
Le Journal d'Alexandrie et la
    bourse égyptienne, 18
Le Journal d'Alger, 2
Le Journal d'Egypte, 22
Le Journal de l'Île de la Réunion, 86

Le Journal de Madagascar, 55
Le Journal de Tanger, 72
Journal du commerce et de la marine, 18
Le Journal du commerce et des
  affaires, 63
Le Journal égyptien, 22
Jugoslovenski glasnik, 22
al-Jumhūrīyah (Cairo), 22
al-Jumhūrīyah (Oran), 4

K

Kalisoliiso, 120
Kampala guardian, 121
KaNgwane times, 104
al-Kawālīs, 70
Kawkab al-Sharq, 22
Kenya daily mail, 42
Kenya daily mail; weekly ed., 42
Kenya mirror, 44
Kenya times, 44
Kenya weekly news, 45
al-Kifāḥ, 52
al-Kifāḥ al-waṭanī, 65
Kinyamateka, 87
Kiongozi, 114
Kodheyo?, 120
Kolo, 58
al-Kūrah, 22
Kurdifān, 1'08
Kusare dunganya, 114
Kweli ikidhihiri uwongo hujitenga, 115
Kweupe, 115

L

Ladybrand courant and border
  herald, 103
Lagazet lalit de klas, 63
Lakroan'i Madagasikara, 58
Die Landstem, 96
Leader, 97
Leselinyana la Lesotho, 46
Lesotho news, 46
Lesotho times, 46
Lesotho weekly, 46
Liberia herald (b-w), 48
Liberia herald (m), 48
Liberia herald (w), 48
Liberian age, 48
Liberian inaugural, 48
Liberian news, 48
Liberian press, 48
Liberian star, 48

Libyan times, 50
Lisān al-'Arab, 22
Liseli, 130
Listener, 48
Livingstone mail, 129
al-Liwā' al-Misrī, 22
O Lobito, 5
Lourenço Marques guardian, 75
Lumiere, 58
Lumiere et paix, 31

M

al-Ma'āhid al-'ulyā: jarīdat
  al-ṭalabah, 23
Madagascar matin, 56
Madagasikara mahaleotena, 56
Madagasikara-1947, 56
Madagasikara-rahampitso, 56
Mafeking mail, 103
Maghreb informations, 65
al-Maghrib, 70
al-Maghrib al-'Arabī, 70
Mahiratra, 56
Malagasy mitolona, 56
Malaŵi news, 59
Mambenga, 126
al-Ma'rakah, 70
Maresaka, 56
Maroc demain, 65
Maroc informations, 66
Maroc-presse, 66
Maroc-presse; American ed., 66
Le Maroc quotidien- la presse
  marocaine, 67
Maroc-soir, 66
Marruecos, 73
al-Masā', 23
al-Masīrah al-khaḍrā', 66
Le Matin du Sahara, 70
Le Mauricien, 63
Mauritius times, 63
al-Mawqif al-usbū'ī, 73
al-Maydān, 52
Mbuga, 121
Mediterranean courier, 66
Le Messager, 23
Mhalamhala, 98
Middle Belt herald, 80
Le Militant, 63
Mirror, 37
Miṣr, 23
Miṣr al-Fatāḥ, 23
Miṣr al-Kinānah, 23
al-Misrī, 23

al-Mīthāq al-Islāmī, 108
al-Mīthāq al-waṭanī, 70
Mjumbe, 128
Mochochonono, 46
Moeletsi oa Basotho, 46
Mombasa advertiser, 42
Mombasa times, 42
Moniteur algérien, 2
Le Moniteur égyptien, 18
Morning news, 108
Morning post, 78
Moroccan courier, 66
Moto, 132
El-Moudjahid, 2
Mseto, 44
Mubaka, 121
al-Muharrir (Casablanca), 66
al-Muharrir (Rabat), 70
al-Mujāhid, 2
al-Mujtamaʻ, 23
Munnansi, 121
Munnansi. English ed., 121
Munno, 121
al-Muqaṭṭam, 23
al-Mushīr, 23
Mutende, 129
Muzinge, 121
Mwafrika, 112
Mwanga, 128
Mwangaza, 112
Mwanger u Tiv, 85
Mwebembezi, 121
Mweti, 15
Mwongozi, 115
Myoto, 126
Mzalendo, 112

N

Nairobi times, 44
Najmat Uktūbar, 92
Nakuru advertiser, 45
Nakuru weekly news, 45
Naledi ya batswana, 100
Namib times, 106
al-Nās, 108
al-Naṣr, 3
Natal daily news, 97
Natal mercury, 97
Natal witness, 104
Nation (Banjul), 34
Nation (Freetown), 91
Nation (Johannesburg), 100
Nation (Port-Louis), 63
Nation (Victoria), 90

La Nation Djibouti, 17
National concord, 80
National observer, 133
Nationalist (Dar es Salaam), 113
Nationalist (Lagos), 82
Native mirror, 132
Neos syndesmos, 27
New age, 96
New Liberian, 49
New Nigerian, 81
New star, 133
Newcastle advertiser, 104
Newcastle morning herald and miners'
    advocate, 104
Ngabo, 121
Ngurumo, 113
al-Nidāʾ, 108
al-Niḍāl (Casablanca), 66
al-Niḍāl (Rabat), 70
Nigeria standard, 80
Nigeria voice, 83
Nigerian chronicle, 78
Nigerian citizen, 85
Nigerian daily record, 79
Nigerian daily sketch, 79
Nigerian daily times, 82
Nigerian eastern mail, 78
Nigerian herald, 80
Nigerian mercantile guardian, 82
Nigerian mirror, 83
Nigerian observer (Benin), 78
Nigerian observer (Port Harcourt), 84
Nigerian outlook, 79
Nigerian spokesman, 83
Nigerian statesman (Lagos), 82
Nigerian statesman (Owerri), 83
Nigerian tide, 84
Nigerian tribune, 79
Nigerian weekly record, 78
Nile mirror, 107
Nile pilot, 108
Nô Pintcha, 40
Northern Natal courier, 97
Northern news, 130
Northern star (Kano), 81
Northern star (Lusaka), 130
Notícias, 75
Notícias da Beira, 74
Notícias de Cabo Verde, 12
La Nouvelle marche, 116
Les Nouvelles, 3
Nsambi, 125
Nsango ya bisu, 126
Ny Gazety Malagasy, 56
Ny marina, 56
Ny Rariny ihany, 56

Nyanza times, 44
Nyasaland times, 59

O

L'Observateur (Cairo), 24
L'Observateur (Ouagadougou), 124
October star, 93
Omukulembeze, 121
Ons land, 104
Ons Vaderland, 102
L'Opinion, 70
L'Ora di Tripoli, 52
Oran républicain, 4
L'Organisation, 62

P

Palaver, 37
Paris-Dakar, 89
Ho Paroikas, 24
La Patrie, 24
People (Freetown), 91
People (Kampala), 122
People (Victoria), 90
People's world, 94
Le Petit journal de Brazzaville, 15
Le petit marocain; le progrès
    marocain, 67
Le petit matin, 118
Le Peuple (Algiers), 3
Le Peuple (Nouakchott), 61
Le Peuple (Port-Louis), 63
Le Peuple (Saint-Denis), 86
Le Phare égyptien, 18
Phos, 24
Pioneer, 38
O Planalto, 5
Le Populaire, 63
Post (Accra), 37
Post (Durban), 97
Post (Johannesburg), 100
Présence congolaise, 126
Press. 104
La Presse d'aujourd'hui:
    Bangui la so, 13
La Presse de Tunisie, 118
La Presse du Cameroun, 10
La Presse marocaine, 67
La Presse marocaine; le
    Maroc quotidien, 67
Pretoria news, 105
Le Progrès (Kinshasa), 126
Le Progrès (Saint-Denis), 86

Progrès-dimanche, 24
Le Progrès égyptien, 24
Le Progrès socialiste, 31
Progress, 96
A Provincia de Angola, 6
Punch, 80

Q

al-Qāfilah/Caravan, 24
al-Qāhirah, 24
al-Qanāh, 27
Il Quotidiano Eritreo, 32
Le Quotidien de la Réunion et de
    l'Ocean Indien, 86
al-Qūwāt al-musallahah (Cairo), 24
al-Qūwāt al-musallahah
    (Khartoum), 108

R

Le Radical, 62
al-Rā'id, 52
Rand daily mail, 100
Rapport, 100
al-Raqīb, 50
Le Rassemblement, 63
al-Ra'y (Tripoli), 52
al-Ra'y (Tunis), 118
al-Ra'y al'Āmm (Cairo), 24
al-Ra'y al'Āmm (Khartoum), 108
Réalités malgaches, 56
La Réforme, 18
La Réforme illustrée du dimanche, 19
La Relève, 87
Renaissance, 79
Le Renouveau du Burundi, 9
Die Republikein, 76
La République, 4
La Réveil, 25
Le Réveil de Djibouti, 17
Revolisiona Malagasy, 57
Rhodesia herald (d), 133
Rhodesia herald (w), 133
Risālat al-Maghrib, 71
Le Rodriguais, 64
Rukwa ruka, 114
Rustenburg herald, 105

S

S. African Jewish times, 100
al-Sa'adah, 71

Saba saba, 122
al-Sabāh, 118
al-Sadá, 118
al-Sadāqah, 25
Sahara libre, 3
Le Sahel, 77
Sahel hebdo, 77
Sahrā' unā, 71
Sahy, 57
Sakaiza, 57
al-Salām (Khartoum), 108
al-Salām (Tunis), 118
Salongo, 126
Samachar, 115
Sandton chronicle, 100
al-Sarāhah, 108
Sareto 'adar, 31
Saturday chronicle, 49
Sauti ya Kanu, 44
Sauti ya Mwafrika, 44
Sawt al-Hind, 25
Sawt al-jāmi'ah, 25
Sawt al-Maghrib, 71
Sawt al-sha'b al-Lībī, 25
Sawt al-Shabāb, 108
Sawt al-Sūdān, 109
Sawt al-Sūmāl, 93
Sawt al-ṭālib/La Voix de l'étudiant, 71
Sawt al-ṭullāb (Cairo), 25
Sawt al-ṭullāb (Khartoum), 109
Sawt al-'ummāl (Cairo), 25
Sawt al-'ummāl (Tripoli), 52
Sawt Hulwān, 25
La Semaine africaine, 16
Il Settimanale Eritreo, 32
Settler, 113
7 jours, 57
Le Seychellois, 90
al-Sha'b (Algiers), 3
al-Sha'b (Cairo), 25
al-Sha'b (Nouakchott), 61
al-Sha'b (Rabat), 71
al-Sha'b (Tripoli), 52
al-Sha'b (Tunis), 118
al-Shabāb, 71
al-Shabāb al-'Arabī, 25
Shabāb al-Azhar, 26
al-Shabāb al-ishtirākī, 28
al-Shu'lah, 50
al-Shurṭī, 52
Sierra Leone daily mail, 91
Sierra Leone guardian, 91
Sierra Leone weekly news, 91
Sierra Leonean, 91
al-Sihāfah (Cairo), 26
al-Sihāfah (Khartoum), 109

al-Sihāfah (Rabat), 71
al-Sinimā wa-al-funūn, 26
al-Siyāsah, 26
al-Siyāsah al-Usbū'īyah, 26
al-Siyāsī, 26
Sodangi kano, 85
Le Soir, 57
Le Soleil, 89
Somali news, 93
Somalia courier; Corriere della
    Somalia, 93
Somaliland news, 92
Le Soudan français, 60
Soukoula, 13
South African Advertiser and mail, 96
South African commercial advertiser, 96
South African financial gazette, 100
South African news, 96
South African worker, 102
South-Western star, 129
Sowetan, 100
Spectator daily, 37
Springs and Brakpan advertiser, 105
Standard (Dar es Salaam), 113
Standard (Nairobi), 44
Le Stanleyvillois, 127
Star (Johannesburg), 101
Star (Kampala), 122
Star (Port-Louis), 64
Stella d'Ottobre, 93
Sudan daily, 109
Sudan daily times, 109
Sudan echo, 109
Sudan news, 109
Sudan standard (d), 109
Sudan standard (s-w), 109
Sudan star, 109
Die Süidwes-Afrikaner, 76
Die Süidwester, 76
Sun, 96
Sunday express (Johannesburg), 101
Sunday express (Lagos), 82
Sunday Ghibli, 53
Sunday mail, 134
Sunday mirror, 37
Sunday nation (Nairobi), 44
Sunday nation (Port-Louis), 64
Sunday news, 113
Sunday people, 80
Sunday post (Johannesburg), 101
Sunday post (Lagos), 82
Sunday post (Nairobi), 45
Sunday standard, 45
Sunday star, 64
Sunday times (Johannesburg), 101

Sunday times (Kampala), 122
Sunday times (Lagos), 83
Sunday times of Zambia, 131
Sunday tribune, 98
Sunday voice, 122
Swazi observer, 111

T

al-Taʿāwun, 26
Taʿāwun al-talabah, 26
al-Taʿāwun: Jarīdat al-Fallāḥīn, 26
Tachydromos, 19
al-Taḥrīr (Casablanca), 67
al-Taḥrīr (Tripoli), 53
Taifa, 128
Taifa empya, 122
Taifa Kenya, 45
Taifa Uganda empya, 122
Taifa weekly, 45
Taifaleo, 45
Takariva isan' andro, 57
al-Talīʿah (Mogadishu), 93
al-Talīʿah (Tripoli), 53
al-Tālib, 53
Tana-journal, 57
Tanganyika opinion, 113
Tanganyika post, 112
Tanganyika standard (d), 113
Tanganyika standard (w), 113
Tanganyika times (d), 113
Tanganyika times (w), 113
Tangier gazette and Morocco mail.
   French ed., 72
Tangier gazette and Morocco mail.
   Spanish ed., 72
Tangier gazette and times of
   Morocco, 73
Ṭarāblus al-Gharb, 53
Tchahakir, 26
El Telegrama del Rif, 68
Le Télégramme algérien, 3
Telonohorefy, 57
Témoignage Chrétien de la Réunion, 86
Témoignages, 86
Le Temps, 118
Temps nouveau d'Afrique, 9
Terre Africaine, 13
Territorial news, 105
al-Thawrah (Khartoum), 110
al-Thawrah (Tripoli), 53
al-Thawrah wa-al-ʿamal, 3
Therisanyo/Consultation, 8
Thohoyandou, 105

al-Tilighrāf, 110
Times (Blantyre), 59
Times (Monrovia), 49
Times of Egypt, 27
Times of Morocco, 73
Times of Swaziland, 111
Times of Zambia, 131
Le Togo français, 116
Togo presse, 116
Le Togo républicain, 116
Tolom-bahoaka, 57
Die Transvaler, 101
A Tribuna, 75
La Tribune Africaine, 126
La Tribune de Madagascar et
   dépendances, 57
La Tribune de Tanger, 73
Truth, 83
Truth prevails where lies must
   vanish, 115
Tselatra, 57
al-Ṭullāb, 27
Tunis hebdo, 118
Tunis-midi, 118
Tunis-soir, 119
La Tunisie française, 119
Tunisie-France, 119

U

Uasin Gishu weekly advertiser, 42
Uganda argus, 122
Uganda eyogera, 122
Uganda nation, 122
Uganda news, 123
Uganda pilot, 123
Uganda post, 123
Uganda times, 123
Uganda weekly news, 123
Uhuru, 114
Ukombozi, 115
Uktūbar 21, 110
Umafrika, 103
al-Ummah (Benghazi), 50
al-Ummah (Khartoum), 110
al-ʿUmmāl (Cairo), 27
al-ʿUmmāl (Casablanca), 67
Umoja, 127
Umsebenzi; South African worker, 102
Umteteli wa Bantu, 102
Umthunywa, 106
União, 75
Unidad de la Guinea Ecuatorial, 29
L'Union, 33
Unity, 91

Urusi leo, 114
al-Usbū', 71

V

Die Vaderland, 102
Vanguard, 34
Vérité, 89
La Vie economique, 71
La Vigie marocaine, 67
Vitoria certa, 6
Voice, 102
Voice of Africa, 45
Voice of Ethiopia, 31
Voice of Uganda, 123
La Voix de l'orient, 27
La Voix du Katanga, 128
Die Volksblad, 94
Die Volkstem, 105
Voz africana, 74
Voz da Guine, 40
A Voz de S. Tomé, 88
Voz di povo, 12
A Voz do Bié, 5
O Voz do planalto, 5
Vryheid gazette and district news, 106
Die Vrystater, 94

W

al-Wafd al-Misrī, 27
al-Waḥdah, 93
War Somali Sidihi, 92
al-Waṭan, 71
Waṭanī, 27
al-Wa'y, 28
We Yone, 91
De Week, 127
Week-end daily news, 98
Weekend news, 49
Weekend star, 45
Weekend world (Johannesburg), 102
Weekend world (Lusaka), 130
Week-ender, 10

Weekly focus, 83
Weekly mirror, 49
Weekly spectator, 37
Weekly topic, 123
Weekly walker, 123
West African monitor, 37
West African pilot, 84
Whirlwind, 49
Windhoek advertiser, 76
Windhoek observer, 76
World, 102
Wynberg times and South African
   agriculturist, 106

X

Xiddigta Oktoobar, 93

Y

'Yancin dan adam, 80
al-Yawm, 53
Yazāréyutu 'Ityoṗyā, 31

Z

al-Ẓāhir, 27
al-Zamān, 50
Zambezi news, 129
Zambia daily mail, 130
Zambia evening mail, 130
Zambia mail, 130
Zambia news, 131
Zambia star, 130
Zanzibar times, 115
Zanzibar voice, 115
Zava, 58
Zava misy, 57
Zimbabwe times, 134
Zuhra, 114
Zululand star, 98
Zululand times, 98